AUDIT GUIDE

Analytical Procedures

WITH CONFORMING CHANGES AS OF

MARCH 1, 2012

[T]his edition of the AICPA Audit Guide *Analytical Procedures*, which was originally issued in 1988, has been modified by [t]he AICPA staff to include certain changes necessary because of the issuance of authoritative guidance since the guide [w]as originally issued. The schedule of changes identifies all changes made in this edition of the guide. The changes [d]o *not* include all those that might be considered necessary if the guide was subjected to a comprehensive review and [r]evision.

11576-359

AICPA®

American Institute of Certified Public Accountants, Inc.
New York, NY 10036-8775

1 2 3 4 5 6 7 8 9 0 AAP 1 9 8 7 6 5 4 3 2

ISBN 978-1-93735-059-8

Important Notice to Reader

This AICPA Audit Guide has been fully conformed to reflect the new standards resulting from the Clarity Project. This year's edition of the guide fully incorporates the clarified auditing standards into all guide content, so that auditors can further their understanding of the clarified auditing standards, as well as begin updating their audit methodologies, resources, and tools prior to the clarified auditing standards' effective date. Additionally, this approach gives auditors the opportunity to review and understand the changes made by their third-party audit methodology and resource providers, if applicable. The clarified auditing standards are effective for audits of financial statements for periods ending on or after December 15, 2012 (calendar year 2012 audits). Auditors should continue to use the March 1, 2008, edition of this guide until the clarified auditing standards become effective for the auditors' engagements.

Preface

About AICPA Audit Guides

This AICPA Audit Guide has been developed by the AICPA Analytical Procedures Working Group to assist practitioners in performing and reporting on their audit engagements.

Auditing guidance included in an AICPA Audit Guide is recognized as an interpretive publication as defined in AU-C section 200, *Overall Objectives of the Independent Auditor and the Conduct of an Audit in Accordance with Generally Accepted Auditing Standards* (AICPA, *Professional Standards*). Interpretive publications are recommendations on the application of generally accepted auditing standards (GAAS) in specific circumstances, including engagements for entities in specialized industries.

An interpretive publication is issued under the authority of the AICPA Auditing Standards Board (ASB) after all ASB members have been provided an opportunity to consider and comment on whether the proposed interpretive publication is consistent with GAAS. The members of the ASB have found the auditing guidance in this guide to be consistent with existing GAAS.

Although interpretive publications are not auditing standards, AU-C section 200 requires the auditor to consider applicable interpretive publications in planning and performing the audit because interpretive publications are relevant to the proper application of GAAS in specific circumstances. If the auditor does not apply the auditing guidance in an applicable interpretive publication, the auditor should document how the requirements of GAAS were complied with in the circumstances addressed by such auditing guidance.

Purpose and Applicability

This guide includes illustrations that demonstrate the importance of forming expectations and considering the precision of the expectation, two of the most misunderstood concepts when applying analytical procedures. The concepts discussed are applicable for all three stages of the audit (planning, substantive testing, and review). However, this guide focuses principally on how the concepts are applied to substantive testing because in designing substantive procedures, auditors ordinarily desire a specified level of audit assurance.

Recognition

Darrel R. Schubert
Chair, ASB

Analytical Procedures Audit Guide Revision Task Force (2000–2001)

Charles E. Landes
O. Ray Whittington

Analytical Procedures Working Group (1996–1998)

George Patterson, *Chair*
Edward Blocher
John A. Fogarty
Stephen D. Holton
Linda S. McDaniel

AICPA Staff

Christopher Cole
Technical Manager,
Accounting and Auditing Publications

Guidance Considered in This Edition

This edition of the guide has been modified by the AICPA staff to include certain changes necessary due to the issuance of authoritative guidance since the guide was originally issued, and other revisions as deemed appropriate. Authoritative guidance issued through March 1, 2012, has been considered in the development of this edition of the guide.

Authoritative guidance that is issued and effective for entities with fiscal years ending on or before March 1, 2012, is incorporated directly in the text of this guide. The presentation of authoritative guidance issued but not yet effective as of March 1, 2012, for entities with fiscal years ending after that same date is being presented differently than in past editions of this guide. This information is being presented as a guidance update, which is a shaded area that contains information related to the new guidance. The distinct presentation of this content is intended to aid the reader in differentiating content that may not be effective for the reader's purposes.

This guide includes relevant guidance issued up to and including the following:

- Statement on Auditing Standards (SAS) No. 125, *Alert That Restricts the Use of the Auditor's Written Communication*, (AICPA, *Professional Standards*, AU-C sec. 905)
- Interpretation No. 1, "Dating the Auditor's Report on Supplementary Information," of AU section 551, *Supplementary Information in Relation to the Financial Statements as a Whole* (AICPA, *Professional Standards*, AU sec. 9551 par. .01–.04)
- Revised interpretations issued through March 1, 2012, including Interpretation No. 1, "Use of Electronic Confirmations," of AU section 330, *The Confirmation Process* (AICPA, *Professional Standards*, AU sec. 9330 par. .01–.08)
- Statement of Position 09-1, *Performing Agreed-Upon Procedures Engagements That Address the Completeness, Accuracy, or Consistency of XBRL-Tagged Data* (AICPA, *Technical Practice Aids*, AUD sec. 14,440)

Users of this guide should consider guidance issued subsequent to those items listed previously to determine their effect on entities covered by this guide. In determining the applicability of recently issued guidance, its effective date should also be considered.

The changes made to this edition of the guide are identified in the schedule of changes appendix. The changes do not include all those that might be considered necessary if the guide were subjected to a comprehensive review and revision.

References to *Professional Standards*

In citing GAAS and their related interpretations, references use section numbers within the codification of currently effective SASs and not the original statement number, as appropriate.

Defining Professional Responsibilities in AICPA *Professional Standards*

AICPA professional standards applicable to audit engagements use the following two categories of professional requirements, identified by specific terms, to describe the degree of responsibility they impose on auditors:

- *Unconditional requirements*. The auditor must comply with an unconditional requirement in all cases in which such requirement is relevant. GAAS use the word *must* to indicate an unconditional requirement.
- *Presumptively mandatory requirements*. The auditor must comply with a presumptively mandatory requirement in all cases in which such a requirement is relevant except in rare circumstances. GAAS use the word *should* to indicate a presumptively mandatory requirement.

In rare circumstances, the auditor may judge it necessary to depart from a relevant presumptively mandatory requirement. In such circumstances, the auditor should perform alternative audit procedures to achieve the intent of that requirement. The need for the auditor to depart from a relevant presumptively mandatory requirement is expected to arise only when the requirement is for a specific procedure to be performed and, in the specific circumstances of the audit, that procedure would be ineffective in achieving the intent of the requirement.

Prior to SAS No. 122, *Statements on Auditing Standards: Clarification and Recodification* (AICPA, *Professional Standards*), the phrase *is required to* or *requires* was used to express an unconditional requirement in GAAS (equivalent to *must*). With the issuance of SAS No. 122, the phrases *is required to* and *requires* does not convey a requirement or the degree of responsibility it imposes on auditors. Instead those terms are used to express that a requirement exists. The terms are typically used in the clarified auditing standards to indicate that a requirement exists elsewhere in GAAS.

AICPA.org Website

The AICPA encourages you to visit the website at www.aicpa.org, and the new Financial Reporting Center at www.aicpa.org/FRC. The Financial Reporting Center was created to support members in the execution of high-quality financial reporting. Whether you are a financial statement preparer or a member in public practice, this center provides exclusive member-only resources for the entire financial reporting process, and provides timely and relevant news, guidance and examples supporting the financial reporting process, including accounting, preparing financial statements and performing compilation, review, audit, attest or assurance and advisory engagements. Certain content on the AICPA's websites referenced in this guide may be restricted to AICPA members only.

Select Recent Developments Significant to This Guide

ASB's Clarity Project

To address concerns over the clarity, length, and complexity of its standards, the ASB has made a significant effort to clarify the SASs. The ASB established clarity drafting conventions and undertook to redraft all of its SASs in accordance with those conventions, which include the following:

- Establishing objectives for each clarified SAS
- Including a definitions section, where relevant, in each clarified SAS
- Separating requirements from application and other explanatory material
- Numbering application and other explanatory material paragraphs using an A- prefix and presenting them in a separate section that follows the requirements section
- Using formatting techniques, such as bulleted lists, to enhance readability
- Including, when appropriate, special considerations relevant to audits of smaller, less complex entities within the text of the clarified SAS
- Including, when appropriate, special considerations relevant to audits of governmental entities within the text of the clarified SAS

In addition, as the ASB redrafted standards for clarity, it also converged the standards with the International Standards on Auditing (ISA), issued by the International Auditing and Assurance Standards Board. As part of redrafting the standards, they now specify more clearly the objectives of the auditor and the requirements which the auditor has to comply with when conducting an audit in accordance with GAAS.

With the release of SAS Nos. 117–120 and Nos. 122–125, the project is near completion. As of the date of this guide, the only SASs remaining to be clarified are

- SAS No. 59, *The Auditor's Consideration of an Entity's Ability to Continue as a Going Concern*, as amended; and
- SAS No. 65, *The Auditor's Consideration of the Internal Audit Function in an Audit of Financial Statements*.

Note that SAS No. 122 withdraws SAS No. 26, *Association With Financial Statements*, as amended, from *Professional Standards*.

SAS Nos. 122–125 will be effective for audits of financial statements for periods ending on or after December 15, 2012. Refer to individual AU-C sections for specific effective date language.

As part of the clarity project, current AU section numbers have been renumbered based on equivalent ISAs. Guidance is located in "AU-C" section numbers instead of "AU" section numbers. "AU-C" is a temporary identifier to avoid confusion with references to existing "AU" sections, which remain effective through 2013, in AICPA *Professional Standards*. The "AU-C" identifier will revert to "AU" in 2014, by which time the clarified auditing standards become fully effective for all engagements. Note that AU-C section numbers for clarified SASs with no equivalent ISAs have been assigned new numbers. The ASB believes that this recodification structure will aid firms and practitioners that use both ISAs and GAAS.

All auditing interpretations corresponding to a SAS have been considered in the development of a clarified SAS and incorporated accordingly, and have been withdrawn by the ASB except for certain interpretations that the ASB has retained and revised to reflect the issuance of SAS No. 122. The effective date of the revised interpretations aligns with the effective date of the corresponding clarified SAS.

Important Notice to Reader

This Audit Guide has been fully conformed to reflect the new standards resulting from the Clarity Project. This year's edition of the guide fully incorporates the clarified auditing standards into all guide content, so that auditors can further their understanding of the clarified auditing standards, as well as begin updating their audit methodologies, resources, and tools prior to the clarified auditing standards' effective date. Additionally, this approach gives auditors the opportunity to review and understand the changes made by their third-party audit methodology and resource providers, if applicable. The clarified auditing standards are effective for audits of financial statements for periods ending on or after December 15, 2012 (calendar year 2012 audits). Auditors should continue to use the March 1, 2008, edition of this guide until the clarified auditing standards become effective for the auditors' engagements.

See the previous section "Guidance Considered in this Edition" for more information related to the guidance issued as of the date of this guide. See also appendix C , "Mapping and Summarization of Changes—Clarified Auditing Standards." This appendix cross references extant AU sections with AU-C sections and indicates the nature of changes made in the clarified standard.

Applicability of Generally Accepted Auditing Standards, the Requirements of the Sarbanes-Oxley Act of 2002, and PCAOB Standards

Audits of the financial statements of *nonissuers* (those entities not subject to the Sarbanes-Oxley Act of 2002 or the rules of the Securities and Exchange Commission [SEC]—that is, private entities, generally speaking) are conducted in accordance with GAAS, as issued by the ASB, the senior technical committee of the AICPA with the authority to promulgate auditing standards for nonissuers. The ASB develops and issues standards in the form of SASs through a due process that includes deliberation in meetings open to the public, public exposure of proposed SASs, and a formal vote. The SASs and their related interpretations are codified in the AICPA's *Professional Standards*. Rule 202, *Compliance With Standards* (AICPA, *Professional Standards*, ET sec. 202 par. .01), of the Code of Professional Conduct requires adherence to the applicable generally accepted auditing standards promulgated by the ASB.

For audits of a nonissuer, in accordance with both GAAS and Public Company Accounting Oversight Board (PCAOB) standards, paragraph .42 of AU-C section 700, *Forming an Opinion and Reporting on Financial Statements* (AICPA, *Professional Standards*), provides reporting guidance applicable to such engagements.

Definition of an Issuer

The Sarbanes-Oxley Act of 2002 states that the term *issuer* means an issuer as defined in Section 3 of the Securities Exchange Act of 1934 (*Commerce and Trade*, *U.S. Code* [USC] 15, Section 78c), the securities of which are registered under Section 12 of that act (15 USC. 781), or that is required to file reports under Section 15(d) (15 USC 78o[d]), or that files or has filed a registration statement that has not yet become effective under the Securities Act of 1933 (15 USC 77a et seq.), and that it has not withdrawn.

Issuers and other entities, when prescribed by the rules of the SEC (collectively referred to in this guide as issuers or issuer), and their public accounting firms which must be registered with the PCAOB are subject to the provisions of the

Sarbanes-Oxley Act of 2002, implementing SEC regulations, and the rules and standards of the PCAOB, as appropriate. The provisions of the Sarbanes-Oxley Act of 2002, the regulations of the SEC, and the rules and standards of the PCAOB are numerous and not all addressed in this section or guide. The SEC has oversight authority over the PCAOB, including the approval of its rules, standards, and budget.

This guide primarily discusses auditing guidance issued by the ASB that applies to nonissuers. Issuers include registered investment companies and audits of issuers are required to be performed under PCAOB standards. Additionally, the Dodd-Frank Wall Street Reform and Consumer Protection Act amends the Sarbanes-Oxley Act of 2002 to give the PCAOB full oversight authority over audits of all broker-dealers (including nonissuers), which includes standard setting, inspection, and enforcement. PCAOB oversight includes a provision that audits of nonissuer broker-dealers are to be conducted in accordance with PCAOB auditing standards. Users should evaluate their audit engagements to determine which auditing standards are applicable.

Guidance for Issuers

Management Assessment of Internal Control

As directed by Section 404 of the Sarbanes-Oxley Act of 2002, the SEC adopted final rules requiring companies subject to the reporting requirements of the Securities Exchange Act of 1934, other than registered investment companies and certain other entities, to include in their annual reports a report from management on the company's internal control over financial reporting. Business development companies, however, do not fall within the scope exception contained in Section 405 and are required to include a report from management on the company's internal control over financial reporting. The SEC rules clarify that management's assessment and report is limited to internal control over financial reporting. The SEC's definition of *internal control* encompasses the Committee of Sponsoring Organizations of the Treadway Commission (COSO) definition, but the SEC does not mandate that the entity use COSO as its criteria for judging effectiveness.

As established by Rule 12b-2 of the Securities Exchange Act of 1934, the auditor's attestation for large accelerated and accelerated filers is currently effective. However, Section 404(c) of the Sarbanes-Oxley Act of 2002 provides that an attestation report of a registered public accounting firm on internal control over financial reporting is not required for an issuer that is neither an accelerated filer nor a large accelerated filer.

Guidance for Auditors

The Sarbanes-Oxley Act of 2002 mandates a number of requirements concerning auditors of issuers, including mandatory registration with the PCAOB, and the setting of auditing standards, inspections, investigations, disciplinary proceedings, prohibited activities, partner rotation, and reports to audit committees, among others. The PCAOB continues to establish rules and standards implementing provisions of the Sarbanes-Oxley Act of 2002 concerning the auditors of issuers.

Applicability of GAAS and PCAOB Standards

Subject to SEC oversight, Section 103 of the Sarbanes-Oxley Act of 2002 authorizes the PCAOB to establish auditing and related attestation, quality control, ethics, and independence standards to be used by registered public accounting firms in the preparation and issuance of audit reports for entities subject to the Sarbanes-Oxley Act of 2002 or the rules of the SEC. Accordingly, public accounting firms registered with the PCAOB are required to adhere to all PCAOB standards in the audits of issuers and other entities when prescribed by the rules of the SEC.

For those entities not subject to the Sarbanes-Oxley Act of 2002 or the rules of the SEC, the preparation and issuance of audit reports remain governed by GAAS, as issued by the ASB.

TABLE OF CONTENTS

Chapter 1

The Use of Analytical Procedures

> **©Update 1-1 *Audit*: Clarified Auditing Standards**
>
> The auditing guidance in this guide edition has been conformed to Statement on Auditing Standards (SAS) Nos. 122–125, which were issued in 2011 as part of the Auditing Standards Board's Clarity Project. These clarified SASs are effective for periods ending on or after December 15, 2012. Early application is not permitted. Although extensive, the revisions to generally accepted auditing standards resulting from these clarified SASs do not change many of the requirements found in the auditing standards that they supersede.
>
> To assist auditors and financial reporting professionals in making the transition, this guide includes appendix C, "Mapping and Summarization of Changes—Clarified Auditing Standards," which provides a cross reference of the sections in the superseded auditing standards to the applicable sections in the clarified auditing standards and identifies the changes, either substantive or primarily clarifying in nature, that may affect an auditor's practice or methodology relative to the applicable sections of SAS Nos. 122–125. It also summarizes the changes resulting from the requirements of SAS Nos. 122–125.
>
> The preface of this guide and the Financial Reporting Center on www.aicpa.org provide more information on the Clarity Project. Visit www.aicpa.org/sasclarity.

1.01 This chapter discusses the concepts and definitions found in AU-C section 520, *Analytical Procedures* (AICPA, *Professional Standards*). Also discussed are the four phases of the analytical procedure process: expectation formation, identification, investigation, and evaluation.

1.02 Analytical procedures are a natural extension of the auditor's understanding of the client's business and add to his or her understanding because the key factors that influence the client's business may be expected to affect the client's financial information. Analytical procedures are used in all three stages of the audit. In the planning stage, the purpose of analytical procedures is to assist in planning the nature, timing, and extent of auditing procedures that will be used to obtain audit evidence for specific account balances or classes of transactions.[1] In the substantive testing stage of the audit, the purpose of analytical procedures is to obtain evidence, sometimes in combination with other substantive procedures, to identify misstatements in account balances, and thus to reduce the risk that misstatements will remain undetected. The auditor's reliance on substantive tests to achieve an audit objective related to a particular assertion may be derived from tests of details, from analytical procedures, or from a combination of both. The decision about which procedure or procedures to use to achieve a particular audit objective is based on the auditor's judgment about the expected effectiveness and efficiency of the available procedures. In the overall review stage, the objective of

---

[1] In accordance with paragraph .06 of AU-C section 315, *Understanding the Entity and Its Environment and Assessing the Risks of Material Misstatement* (AICPA, *Professional Standards*), analytical procedures should be performed as risk assessment procedures to provide a basis for the identification and assessment of risks of material misstatement at the financial statement and relevant assertion levels. Refer to AU-C section 315 for further guidance.

analytical procedures is to assist the auditor in assessing the conclusions reached and in evaluating the overall financial statement presentation.

Concepts and Definitions

Analytical Procedures

1.03 Analytical procedures are defined by paragraph .04 of AU-C section 520 as "evaluations of financial information through analysis of plausible relationships among both financial and nonfinancial data. Analytical procedures also encompass such investigation, as is necessary, of identified fluctuations or relationships that are inconsistent with other relevant information or that differ from expected values by a significant amount." The definition implies several key concepts:

- The "evaluations of financial information" suggests that analytical procedures will be used to understand or test financial statement relationships or balances.
- The "investigation...of identified fluctuations or relationships that are inconsistent with other relevant information or that differ from expected values by a significant amount" implies an understanding of what can reasonably be expected and involves a comparison of the recorded book values with an auditor's expectations and an understanding of those differences.
- "Relationships among both financial and nonfinancial data" suggests that both types of data can be useful in understanding the relationships of the financial information and, therefore, in forming an expectation.

1.04 AU-C section 520 addresses the auditor's use of analytical procedures as substantive procedures (substantive analytical procedures). It also addresses the auditor's responsibility to perform analytical procedures near the end of the audit that assist the auditor when forming an overall conclusion on the financial statements. Analytical procedures also are used as risk assessment procedures (which may be referred to as analytical procedures used to plan the audit), as described in AU-C section 315, *Understanding the Entity and Its Environment and Assessing the Risks of Material Misstatement*, (AICPA, *Professional Standards*). AU-C section 330, *Performing Audit Procedures in Response to Assessed Risks and Evaluating the Audit Evidence Obtained* (AICPA, *Professional Standards*), also addresses the use of analytical procedures as substantive procedures. In all cases, the effectiveness of analytical procedures lies in developing expectations that can reasonably be expected to identify unexpected relationships. Paragraph .08 of AU-C section 520 provides requirements for documentation of the performance of substantive analytical procedures. If an analytical procedure is used as the principal substantive test of a significant financial statement assertion, the auditor should document all of the following:

a. The expectation referred to in paragraph .05*c* of AU-C section 520 and the factors considered in its development when that expectation or those factors are not otherwise readily determinable from the audit documentation

b. Results of the comparison referred to in paragraph .05*d* of AU-C section 520 of the recorded amounts, or ratios developed from recorded amounts, with the expectations *c.* Any additional auditing procedures performed in accordance with paragraph .07 of AU-C section 520 relating to the investigation of fluctuations or relationships that are inconsistent with other relevant information or that differ from expected values by a significant amount and the results of such additional procedures

1.05 Also, in accordance with paragraphs .06*b* and .A7–.A9 of AU-C section 315, the auditor should apply analytical procedures on the planning stage of the audit. Those procedures may provide useful information in planning the audit to assist in understanding the entity and its environment and to identify areas that may represent specific risks relevant to the audit. For example, analytical procedures may be helpful in identifying the existence of unusual transactions or events, and amounts, ratios, and trends that might indicate matters that have financial statement and audit implications. In performing analytical procedures as risk assessment procedures, the auditor should develop expectations about plausible relationships that are reasonably expected to exist. When comparison of those expectations with recorded amounts or ratios developed from recorded amounts yields unusual or unexpected relationships, the auditor should consider those results in identifying risks of material misstatement. However, when such analytical procedures use data aggregated at a high level (which is often the situation), the results of those analytical procedures provide only a broad initial indication about whether a material misstatement may exist. Accordingly, the auditor should consider the results of such analytical procedures along with other information gathered in identifying the risks of material misstatement.

1.06 Analytical procedures performed when forming an overall conclusion about whether the financial statements are consistent with the auditor's understanding of the entity are designed to assist the auditor in assessing (*a*) the adequacy of the evidence gathered in response to unusual or unexpected balances identified during the course of the audit and (*b*) all significant fluctuations and other unusual items have been adequately identified and explained.

1.07 During the substantive testing stage, analytical procedures may be used to obtain assurance that material misstatements are not likely to exist in financial statement account balances. If analytical procedures are used for substantive testing, the auditor should focus his or her analytical procedures on relevant assertions related to each material class of transactions, account balance, and disclosure and should give detailed attention to the underlying factors that affect those areas through the development of an expectation independent of the recorded balance. Therefore, substantive analytical procedures generally are performed with more rigor and precision than those used for planning or overall review.

1.08 Paragraph .05 of AU-C section 520 contains requirements when designing and performing analytical procedures, either alone or in combination with tests of details, as substantive procedures in accordance with AU-C section 330. The auditor should

a. determine the suitability of particular substantive analytical procedures for given assertions, taking into account the assessed risks of material misstatement and tests of details, if any, for these assertions;

b. evaluate the reliability of data from which the auditor's expectation of recorded amounts or ratios is developed, taking into account the source, comparability, and nature and relevance of information available and controls over preparation;

c. develop an expectation of recorded amounts or ratios and evaluate whether the expectation is sufficiently precise (taking into account whether substantive analytical procedures are to be performed alone or in combination with tests of details) to identify a misstatement that, individually or when aggregated with other misstatements, may cause the financial statements to be materially misstated; and

d. determine the amount of any difference of recorded amounts from expected values that is acceptable without further investigation as required by paragraph .07 of AU-C 520 and compare the recorded amounts, or ratios developed from recorded amounts, with the expectations.

When evaluating the reliability of the data, as required in paragraph .05*b* of AU-C section 520, the auditor could test the controls, if any, over the entity's preparation of information to be used by the auditor in applying analytical procedures. When such controls are effective, the auditor has greater confidence in the reliability of the information and, therefore, in the results of analytical procedures. When designing substantive analytical procedures, the auditor should evaluate whether the controls that are in place are operating effectively, including the risk of management override of controls. As part of this process, the auditor might need to evaluate whether such an override might have allowed adjustments outside of the normal period-end financial reporting process to have been made to the financial statements. Such adjustments might have resulted in artificial changes to the financial statement relationships being analyzed, causing the auditor to draw erroneous conclusions. For this reason, substantive analytical procedures alone are not well suited to detecting some types of fraud. Alternatively, the auditor may consider whether the information was subjected to audit testing in the current or prior period. In determining the audit procedures to apply to the information upon which the expectation for substantive analytical procedures is based, the auditor should consider the guidance in paragraphs .07–.10 of AU-C section 500, *Audit Evidence* (AICPA, *Professional Standards*), as it relates to the relevance and reliability of the information.

1.09 In planning substantive analytical procedures, the auditor should consider the amount of difference from the expectation that can be accepted without further investigation. This consideration is influenced primarily by performance materiality and should be consistent with the desired level of assurance. Determination of this amount involves considering the possibility that a combination of misstatements in the specific account balance, class of transactions, or disclosure could aggregate to an unacceptable amount. In designing substantive analytical procedures, the auditor should increase the desired level of assurance as the risk of material misstatement increases.

Expectations

1.10 Expectations are the auditor's predictions of recorded accounts or ratios. In performing analytical procedures, the auditor should develop the expectation in such a way that a significant difference between it and the recorded amount is indicative of a misstatement, unless he or she can obtain and corroborate explanations for the difference (for example, an unusual event occurred). Expectations are developed by identifying plausible relationships (for example, store square footage and retail sales) that are reasonably expected to exist based on the auditor's understanding of the client and of the industry in which the client operates. The auditor may select from a variety of data sources to form expectations. For example, the auditor may use prior-period information (adjusted for expected changes), management's budgets or forecasts, industry data, or nonfinancial data. The source of information determines, in part, the precision with which the auditor predicts an account balance and, therefore, is important to consider in developing an expectation to achieve the desired level of assurance from the analytical procedure.

Precision

1.11 Precision is a measure of the closeness of the auditor's expectation to the correct amount. The desired precision of the expectation varies according to the stage of the audit or the purpose of the analytical procedure. For example, precision is more important for analytical procedures used as substantive tests than for those used in planning. The effectiveness of analytical procedures depends on their precision and purpose. Factors that affect the precision of analytical procedures include

- the type of expectation developed.
- the reliability and other characteristics of the data used in forming the expectation (both internally and externally prepared data).
- the nature of the account or the assertion.

1.12 For example, an auditor plans to test interest income. Because the nature of the account is relatively objective (interest income can easily be predicted), analytical procedures could be designed to serve as an effective substantive test. If the auditor needs a high level of assurance from a procedure, he or she should develop a relatively precise expectation by selecting the appropriate type of expectation (for example, a reasonableness test instead of a simple trend analysis), the level of detail of the data (for example, quarterly versus annual data), and the reliability of the source of the data (for example, data that have been subject to auditing procedures versus data that have not been subject to auditing procedures). In the case of substantive tests, the precision of the expectation is the primary determinant of the level of assurance obtained from the analytical procedure. It affects the ability of the auditor to identify correctly whether a given unexpected difference in an account balance is the result of a misstatement. Because precision is directly related to the level of assurance obtained, it is an important consideration in determining whether the planned level of assurance desired from the analytical procedure is achieved. In addition, the higher the desired levels of assurance, the more precise the expectation would need to be.

Level of Assurance

1.13 Level of assurance is the complement of the level of detection risk and is the degree to which substantive auditing procedures (including analytical procedures) provide evidence in testing an assertion. The level of assurance is dependent on the restriction of detection risk because inherent and control risk exist independently of an audit of financial statements. Detection risk relates to the auditor's procedures and can be changed at his or her discretion. The desired or planned level of assurance is that level needed to achieve an acceptable level of detection risk. It is determined by the acceptable level of audit risk, the risk of material misstatement (in other words, the combined assessment of inherent and control risk), and the planning materiality threshold. The achieved level of assurance is the degree to which the auditing procedure actually reduces audit risk and is a function of the effectiveness of the substantive procedures.

Analytical Procedure Process: Four Phases

1.14 The use of analytical procedures can be considered a process that consists of four phases. The first phase is the expectation-formation process. In this phase, the auditor forms an expectation of an account balance or financial relationship. In doing so, the auditor determines the precision of the expectation and thus, in part, the effectiveness of the analytical procedure.

1.15 The remaining three phases consist of the identification, investigation, and evaluation of the difference between the auditor's expected value and the recorded book value in light of the auditor's materiality assessment. In the second phase, identification, the auditor identifies whether an unusual fluctuation exists between the expected and recorded amounts. In the third, investigation, the auditor investigates the cause of unexpected differences by considering possible causes and searching for information to identify the most probable causes. Finally, in the evaluation phase, the auditor evaluates the likelihood of material misstatement and determines the nature and extent of any additional auditing procedures that may be required.

Expectation Formation (Phase I)

1.16 Forming an expectation is the most important phase of the analytical procedure process. The more precise the expectation (that is, the closer the auditor's expectation is to the correct balance or relationship), the more effective the procedure will be at identifying potential misstatements. Also, paragraph .05*c* of AU-C section 520 states that the expectation should be precise enough to provide the desired level of assurance that differences that may be potential misstatements, individually or when aggregated with other misstatements, would be identified for the auditor to investigate.

1.17 The effectiveness of an analytical procedure is a function of three factors related to the precision with which the expectation is developed: (*a*) the nature of the account or assertion, (*b*) the reliability and other characteristics of the data, and (*c*) the inherent precision of the expectation method used. Following is a discussion about each of these factors.

Nature of the Account or Assertion

1.18 Analytical procedures are based on relationships between data (see appendix A, "Measures of Precision for a Regression Analysis," of this guide), for example, how this year compares with last and how amounts on a balance sheet relate to income and expense items. The more predictable the relationships are, the more precise the expectation will be. The following are factors an auditor may consider in predicting the amount of an account:

- The subjective or objective nature of the items in an account balance (for example, whether the account comprises estimates or the accumulation of transactions)
- Product mix

- Company profile (for example, the number of stores or the various locations)
- Management's discretion (for example, estimates)
- Stability of the environment
- Income statement or balance sheet account

1.19 Numerous factors affect the amount of an account balance. Increasing the number of such factors considered in forming an expectation of the account balance increases the precision of the expectation. Such factors include

- significant events.
- accounting changes.
- business and industry factors.
- market and economic factors.
- management incentives.
- initial versus repeat engagement.

1.20 Moreover, expectations developed for income statement accounts tend to be more precise than expectations for balance sheet accounts because income statement relationships generally are more predictable. In addition, expectations formed under stable economic conditions (for example, stable interest rates) or stable environmental factors (for example, no regulatory changes) tend to be more precise relative to an unstable economy or environment.

Reliability and Other Characteristics of the Data

1.21 In forming an expectation, an auditor should consider two broad factors related to the characteristics of the data included in the account: the level of detail on which the auditor is able to base his or her expectation and the reliability of the data.

1.22 In general, the more disaggregated the data, the more precise the expectation. For example, the use of monthly instead of annual data tends to improve the precision of the expectation. Preparing an expectation by store or division is also more precise than an expectation based on consolidated data.

1.23 The more reliable the source of the data, the more precise the expectation. The following are factors related to the reliability of data that the auditor may consider in forming the expectation:

- *Strength of the company's internal control.* The stronger the internal control over financial reporting (which includes controls over the accounting system), the more reliable the data generated from the company's accounting system.
- *Outside versus internal data and degree of independence.* Data from more objective or independent sources are more reliable (for example, third-party generated versus management generated).
- *Nonfinancial versus financial data or data that has been subject to auditing procedures versus data that has not been subject to auditing procedures.* The use of reliable nonfinancial data (for example, store square footage or occupancy rates) and the use of data that has been subjected to auditing procedures improve the precision of the expectation.

1.24 The auditor should assess the reliability of data used to develop his or her expectations, taking into account, if necessary, the results of other related procedures. When substantive analytical procedures are used to test for both overstatement and understatement, the auditor needs to ensure that the data used to build the expectation is reliable in both directions.

Inherent Precision of the Expectation Method Used

1.25 Expectations can be developed with methods as simple as using the prior-year sales balance (adjusted for expected changes) as the expectation for current year sales or as complex as multiple regression analysis that incorporates both financial (for example, cost of goods sold) and nonfinancial data (for example, store square footage) to predict retail sales. The auditor typically selects the most appropriate type of expectation method to use for an account by considering the level of assurance desired for the procedure. Determining which type of expectation method is appropriate is a matter of professional judgment; however, the inherent precision of the expectation method used is a consideration in developing the expectation. The four types of expectation methods and their appropriateness are discussed in the following paragraphs.

1.26 *Trend analysis.* This is the analysis of changes in an account balance over time. Simple trends typically compare last year's account balance to the current unaudited balance. More sophisticated trends encompass multiple time periods.

1.27 Trend analysis is most appropriate when the account or relationship is fairly predictable (for example, sales in a stable environment). It is less effective when the entity under audit has experienced significant operating or accounting changes. The number of years used in the trend analysis is a function of the stability of operations. The more stable the operations over time, the more predictable the relations and the more appropriate the use of multiple time periods.

1.28 Trend analysis at an aggregate level (for example, trend analysis of an entity's operating units on a consolidated basis) is relatively imprecise because a material misstatement is often small relative to the natural variation in an aggregate account balance. This suggests the need to perform trend analysis on a disaggregated level (for example, by segment, product, or location, and monthly or quarterly rather than on an annual basis).

1.29 In using trend analysis, it is important for the auditor to understand the volatility of the environment related to the accounts being tested. For example, research has shown that, except in situations in which the environment has remained stable relative to the prior year, using only the prior-year balance as the expectation reduces the effectiveness of analytical procedures to identify potential high-risk areas. In fact, using only the prior-year balance without considering whether it is the most appropriate expectation can lead to a bias toward accepting the current data that have not been subject to auditing procedures as fairly stated, even when they are misstated.

1.30 *Ratio analysis.* This is the comparison of relationships between financial statement accounts (between two periods or over time), the comparison of an account with nonfinancial data (for example, revenue per order or sales per square foot), or the comparison of relationships between firms in an industry (for example, gross profit comparisons). Ratio analysis entails a comparison of interrelations between accounts, nonfinancial information, or both. Another example of ratio analysis (which is sometimes referred to as common size analysis) is the comparison of the ratio of shipping costs or other selling expenses to sales from the prior year with the current year ratio, or the comparison of shipping costs to sales with the ratio for a comparable firm in the same industry. See appendix B, "Financial Ratios," of this guide for a listing of helpful ratios.

1.31 Ratio analysis is most appropriate when the relationship between accounts is fairly predictable and stable (for example, the relationship between sales and accounts receivable). Ratio analysis can be more effective than trend analysis because comparisons between the balance sheet and income statement can often reveal unusual fluctuations that an analysis of the individual accounts would not. Comparison of ratios with industry averages (or with comparable firms in the same industry) is most useful when operating factors are comparable.

1.32 Ratio analysis at an aggregate level (that is, consolidated operating units or across product lines) is relatively imprecise because a material misstatement is often small relative to the natural variations in the ratios. This suggests the need to perform ratio analysis on a disaggregated level (for example, by segment, product, or location).

1.33 *Reasonableness testing.* This is the analysis of account balances or changes in account balances within an accounting period that involves the development of an expectation based on financial data, nonfinancial data, or both. For example, an expectation for hotel revenues may be developed using the average occupancy rate, the average room rate for all rooms, or room rate by category or class of room. Also, using the number of employees hired and terminated, the timing of pay changes, and the effect of vacation and sick days, the model could predict the change in payroll expense from the previous year to the current balance within a fairly narrow dollar range.

1.34 In contrast to both trend and ratio analyses (which implicitly assume stable relationships), reasonableness tests use information to develop an explicit prediction of the account balance or relationship of interest. Reasonableness tests rely on the auditor's knowledge of the relationships, including knowledge of the factors that affect the account balances. The auditor uses that knowledge to develop assumptions for each of the key factors (for example, industry and economic factors) to estimate the account balance. A reasonableness test for sales could be explicitly formed by considering the number of units sold, the unit price by product line, different pricing structures, and an understanding of industry trends during the period. This is in contrast to an implicit trend expectation for sales based on last year's sales. The latter expectation is appropriate only if there were no other factors affecting sales during the current year, which is not the usual situation.

1.35 *Regression analysis.* This is the use of statistical models to quantify the auditor's expectation in dollar terms, with measurable risk and precision levels.[2] For example, an expectation for sales may be developed based on management's sales forecast, commission expense, and changes in advertising expenditures.

1.36 Regression analysis is similar to reasonableness testing in that there is an explicit prediction using the auditor's knowledge of the factors that affect

---

[2] In many cases, the client has developed analytical procedures, internal models, or both for monitoring and evaluating its business and performance. The auditor may find these internal analytics useful for developing his or her own analytical procedures in the planning phase of an audit and substantive testing purposes.

the account balances to develop a model of the account balance. The model is most effective when the data are disaggregated and are from an accounting system with effective internal controls.

Relationship Between the Methods Used to Develop an Expectation and the Precision of the Expectation

1.37 Of the four types of expectation methods, trend analysis generally provides the least precision because this expectation method does not take into consideration changes in specific factors that affect the account (for example, product mix). The imprecision is magnified in the context of a changing environment in which the assumptions underlying the prior year numbers are no longer valid. For example, the auditor is predicting sales and new products have been introduced, or economic conditions affecting sales have changed significantly. Using prior year's sales (or an average of the time series) as the implicit expectation for current sales does not provide a precise expectation because it omits relevant information about additional products and changes in the economic environment.[3]

1.38 Regression analysis, in contrast, provides potentially the highest level of precision because an explicit expectation is formed in which the relevant data can be incorporated in a model to predict current year sales. Regression analysis potentially can take into account all of the relevant operating data (sales volume by product), changes in operations (changes in advertising levels, changes in product lines or product mix), and changes in economic conditions. In addition, regression analysis allows the auditor to measure the precision of the expectation.

1.39 The precision of ratio analysis and reasonableness testing typically falls somewhere in between that of trend analysis and regression analysis. However, reasonableness tests generally provide better precision because they involve the formation of explicit expectations similar to regression analysis. That is, reasonableness tests can employ multiple sources of data, both financial and nonfinancial, across time. Ratio analysis is similar to trend analysis in that it employs an implicit expectation. That is, when using a reasonableness test, the auditor may begin with the idea of predicting the balance, whereas for ratio analysis, the expectation formation process is implicit—as the ratio is compared with budget, industry, or other relevant benchmarks.

1.40 Some aspects of the foregoing analysis can be summarized and grouped according to a number of factors, as follows:

- *Explicit or implicit expectation.* When using reasonableness tests or regression, the auditor is explicitly forming an expectation. This approach helps to increase the precision of the expectation. In contrast, in using trend and ratio analysis the auditor may tend to rely more upon comparison and evaluation, for example, to budget, prior year, or industry figures that may or may not be relevant due to changes in the entity's operations or in the economic environment affecting the entity or its specific industry.
- *Number of predictors.* Trend analysis is limited to a single predictor, that is, the prior period's or periods' data for that account. Because

[3] This discussion is not intended to suggest that trend analysis is imprecise or that it cannot be improved to be more precise. For example, changing interest rates, inflation, or price changes can be incorporated or factored into trend analysis to increase the analytical procedure's precision.

ratio analysis employs two or more related financial or nonfinancial sources of information, thus using known relationships among the accounts, the result is a more precise expectation. Reasonableness tests and regression analysis further improve the precision of the expectation by allowing potentially as many variables (financial and nonfinancial) as are relevant for forming the expectation.

- *Operating data.* Trend analysis, by relying on a single predictor, does not allow the use of potentially relevant operating data, as do the other three types of procedures.
- *External data.* Reasonableness tests and regression analysis are able to use external data (for example, general economic and industry data) directly in forming the expectation. Although external data can potentially be used in ratio analysis, its use in this manner is quite rare.
- *Statistical power.* Of the four expectation methods described herein, only regression analysis provides the benefits of statistical precision. The statistical model provides not only a best expectation given the data at hand, but also provides quantitative measures of the fit of the model.

Table 1-1 illustrates how the four expectation methods differ in terms of the five criteria in the previous list for determining the most appropriate method.

Table 1-1

The Relationship Between Types of Analytical Procedures and Selected Precision Factors

Type of Analytical Procedure	*Explicit or Implicit Expectation*	*Number of Predictors*	*Can Include Operating Data*	*Can Include External Data*	*Measure of Statistical Precision*
Trend Analysis	Implicit	One	No	No	No
Ratio Analysis	Implicit	Two	Yes	Limited	No
Reasonableness Test	Explicit	Two or more	Yes	Yes	No
Regression Analysis	Explicit	Two or more	Yes	Yes	Yes

Identification and Investigation (Phases II and III)

1.41 The next two phases of the analytical procedure process consist of identification and investigation. Identification begins by comparing the auditor's expected value with the recorded amount. Given that the auditor developed an expectation with a particular amount of difference that could be accepted without further explanation, he or she then compares the unexpected differences with the threshold. In substantive testing, an auditor testing for the possible misstatement of the book value of an account determines whether the audit difference was less than the auditor's threshold. If the difference is less than the acceptable threshold, taking into consideration the desired level of assurance from the procedure, the auditor accepts the book value without further investigation. If the difference is greater, the next step is to investigate the difference.

1.42 In investigation, the auditor should evaluate possible explanations for the difference. The greater the precision of the expectation (that is, the closer the expectation is to the correct amount), the greater the likelihood that the difference between the expected and recorded amounts is due to misstatement rather than nonmisstatement causes. The difference between an auditor's expectation and the recorded book value of an account (value of an account not subject to auditing procedures) can be due to any or all of the following three causes: (*a*) the difference is due to misstatements, (*b*) the difference is due to inherent factors that affect the account being audited (for example, the predictability of the account or account subjectivity), and (*c*) the difference is due to factors related to the reliability of data used to develop the expectation (for example, data that have been subject to auditing procedures versus data that have not been subject to auditing procedures). The greater the precision of the expectation, the more likely the difference between the auditor's expectation and the recorded value will be due to misstatements (cause *a*). Conversely, the less precise the expectation, the more likely the difference is due to factors related to the precision of the expectation (causes *b* and *c*).

1.43 If the auditor believes that the difference is more likely due to factors related to the precision of the expectation, the auditor should consider whether a more precise expectation can be cost-effectively developed. If so, the analytical procedure should be reperformed based on the new expectation, and the new difference should be calculated. On the other hand, the auditor may rule out causes *b* and *c* (see paragraph 1.42) as explanations for the unexpected difference and may then evaluate the unexpected difference as a potential misstatement. The auditor should then perform further analysis and inquiry to evaluate the most likely causes and identify a plausible explanation.

1.44 Plausible explanations usually relate to unusual transactions or events or accounting or business changes. In evaluating whether an explanation is plausible, the auditor might consider such factors as

- the understanding of matters noted while performing audit work in other areas, particularly while performing audit work on the data used to develop the expectation.
- management and board reports containing explanations of significant variances between budgeted and actual results.
- review of board minutes.
- information on unusual events occurring in prior years (this may indicate the types of unusual events that could have affected the current year data).

1.45 When analytical procedures serve as substantive tests, the auditor should ordinarily corroborate explanations for significant differences by obtaining sufficient appropriate audit evidence. The procedures used to corroborate the explanation depend on the nature of the explanation, the nature of the account balance, and the results of other substantive procedures. To corroborate an explanation, one or more of the following techniques may be used:

- *Inquiries of persons outside the client's organization.* For example, the auditor may confirm discounts received with major suppliers or agree to changes in commodity prices with a commodities exchange or the financial press.

- *Inquiries of independent persons inside the client's organization.* For example, an explanation received from the financial controller for an increase in advertising expenditures might be corroborated with the marketing director. It is normally inappropriate to corroborate explanations only by discussion with other accounting department personnel.
- *Evidence obtained from other auditing procedures.* Sometimes the results of other auditing procedures (particularly those performed on the data used to develop an expectation) are sufficient to corroborate an explanation.
- *Examination of supporting evidence.* The auditor may examine supporting documentary evidence of transactions to corroborate explanations. For example, if an increase in cost of sales in one month was attributed to an unusually large sales contract, the auditor might examine supporting documentation, such as the sales contract and delivery dockets.

1.46 When the population is disaggregated, a pattern in the differences may indicate that there is a common explanation for those differences. However, the auditor cannot assume that this is the case. He or she should perform sufficient work to corroborate each significant difference.

Evaluation (Phase IV)

1.47 The final phase of the analytical procedure process consists of evaluating the difference between the auditor's expected value and the recorded amount. It is usually not practicable to identify factors that explain the exact amount of a difference identified for investigation. However, the auditor should attempt to quantify that portion of the difference for which plausible explanations can be obtained and, where appropriate, corroborated and determine that the amount that cannot be explained is sufficiently small to enable him or her to conclude on the absence of material misstatement.

1.48 If a reasonable explanation cannot be obtained, in accordance with paragraph .11 of AU-C section 450, *Evaluation of Misstatements Identified During the Audit* (AICPA, *Professional Standards*), the auditor should determine whether uncorrected misstatements are material, individually or in the aggregate. In making this determination, the auditor should consider (*a*) the size and nature of the misstatements, both in relation to particular classes of transactions, account balances, or disclosures and the financial statements as a whole, and the particular circumstances of their occurrence and (*b*) the effect of uncorrected misstatements related to prior periods on the relevant classes of transactions, account balances, or disclosures and the financial statements as a whole.

Chapter 2
Questions and Answers

> **©Update 2-1 *Audit*: Clarified Auditing Standards**
>
> The auditing guidance in this guide edition has been conformed to Statement on Auditing Standards (SAS) Nos. 122–125, which were issued in 2011 as part of the Auditing Standards Board's Clarity Project. These clarified SASs are effective for periods ending on or after December 15, 2012. Early application is not permitted. Although extensive, the revisions to generally accepted auditing standards resulting from these clarified SASs do not change many of the requirements found in the auditing standards that they supersede.
>
> To assist auditors and financial reporting professionals in making the transition, this guide includes appendix C, "Mapping and Summarization of Changes—Clarified Auditing Standards," which provides a cross reference of the sections in the superseded auditing standards to the applicable sections in the clarified auditing standards and identifies the changes, either substantive or primarily clarifying in nature, that may affect an auditor's practice or methodology relative to the applicable sections of SAS Nos. 122–125. It also summarizes the changes resulting from the requirements of SAS Nos. 122–125.
>
> The preface of this guide and the Financial Reporting Center on www.aicpa.org provide more information on the Clarity Project. Visit www.aicpa.org/sasclarity.

2.01 This chapter provides questions and answers relating to analytical procedures. The questions and answers are grouped in the following five categories: precision of the expectation, relationship of analytical procedures to the audit risk model, evaluation and investigation, purpose of analytical procedures, and fraud.

Precision of the Expectation

2.02 Question 1: What factors are important in determining the level of assurance provided by an analytical procedure?

2.03 Answer: The level of assurance provided by an analytical procedure is determined by the precision of the expectation. The higher the precision, the greater the level of assurance provided by the procedure. The factors affecting the precision of an expectation are

a. the nature of the account or assertion (for example, its predictability or subjectivity).

b. the characteristics of the data including the level of disaggregation of the data and the availability, sources, and reliability of the data.

c. the inherent precision of the type of expectation formed (trend or ratio analysis, reasonableness test, or regression analysis).

2.04 Question 2: How does the aggregation of data affect the level of assurance provided by an analytical procedure?

2.05 Answer: Data aggregation refers to the level at which account balances are combined for testing (for example, account balances on an annual instead of a quarterly basis or the consolidation of operating units). Generally, the more disaggregated the data used to form the expectation, the more precise that expectation will be. This will result in a higher level of assurance that material misstatement will be detected. Disaggregation is typically more important when the entity's operations are more complex or diversified. However, the auditor should assess the reliability of disaggregated data. For example, certain quarterly data may be less reliable than annual data because it is unaudited or is not subject to the same controls as the annual data. The auditor should use judgment in determining which precision factor is more important in the circumstances. (See the case study in chapter 3, "Case Study: On the Go Stores," of this guide and in paragraph .05 of AU-C section 520, *Analytical Procedures* [AICPA, *Professional Standards*].)

2.06 Question 3: How does the reliability of the data used in forming an expectation affect the level of assurance provided by the analytical procedure?

2.07 Answer: One of the factors affecting the precision of the expectation, and thus the level of assurance, is the reliability of the data sources used to develop the expectation. For example, data that have been subject to auditing procedures are more likely to be reliable than data that have not. If the data are produced by the entity's financial reporting system, the auditor should assess the level of control risk in assessing data reliability (see question 9). If the data are produced by another reporting system within the entity outside the financial reporting function, the auditor should assess the manner in which the data are developed and reviewed by management. If the data are produced outside the entity, the auditor should assess the objectivity of the source (for example, the independence of the publisher of the data from the intended users of the data) and the manner in which they were developed. Examples of matters to consider when evaluating data produced outside the entity include (*a*) the existence of a defined set of measurement criteria, (*b*) observed flaws in previous publications of similar reports, and (*c*) the general acceptance of the data source. For example, statistics published by the U.S. Department of Labor are more likely to be reliable than similar statistics provided by an industry trade group.

2.08 Question 4: What is the role of planning materiality in determining the desired precision of an expectation in testing an account balance?

2.09 Answer: Planning materiality is an indication of the amount of misstatement in the financial statements that an auditor is willing to accept. Planning materiality, in part, determines the level of assurance that the auditor expects to obtain from the audit procedure. Because the precision of the expectation directly affects the level of assurance, the auditor should consider materiality when determining how precise an expectation needs to be to detect misstatements that, in the aggregate, exceed materiality. An inverse relationship exists between the precision of the expectation and planning materiality. Holding all other factors constant, as planning materiality decreases, the expectation becomes more precise to achieve the same level of assurance.

2.10 Question 5: When is it beneficial to form expectations for substantive tests using regression analysis?

2.11 Answer: Regression analysis provides a means of quantifying the assurance obtained that is not available when using other types of analytical procedures. Because of the ability to quantify the precision achieved, regression analysis is beneficial when a high level of assurance is needed from the analytical procedure. It also provides a more rigorous means of quantifying likely errors.

2.12 Question 6: When is it beneficial to form expectations for substantive tests using ratio or trend analysis and reasonableness tests?

2.13 Answer: Ratio and trend analysis are often used in audit planning. However, when plausible and predictable relationships exist between the data used to form the expectation and the balance to be tested, and the data are reliable and disaggregated, ratio and trend analyses can be effective substantive tests. Generally, ratio and trend analyses are relatively imprecise and should be performed at a disaggregated level when higher levels of assurance are desired. Reasonableness tests often are used in testing account balances, particularly estimates, by forming expectations based on financial or nonfinancial data. If a high level of assurance is desired from a reasonableness test (for example, to test a detailed transaction), the auditor often reconstructs or recomputes the balance.

2.14 Question 7: What are the differences, if any, between expectation formation for analytical procedures used during planning, substantive testing, and the overall review stages of the audit?

2.15 Answer: Precision of the expectation is the most important factor in determining the level of assurance the analytical procedure provides. When performing analytical procedures during planning, the primary focus is to identify unexpected changes or the absence of expected changes that may indicate a risk of material misstatement. The purpose of those procedures is to assist in determining the nature, timing, and extent of substantive procedures. As a result, the expectations can be less precise, and the analysis and investigation of unexpected changes can be less extensive. In contrast, when performing analytical procedures as substantive tests, the desired level of assurance is higher than that of the planning stage; therefore, expectations of the recorded amounts should be more precise, because the procedures performed are to directly identify misstatements in the account balances being tested. When performing analytical procedures in the overall review stage of the audit, the focus is on assisting the auditor in assessing the conclusions reached as a result of substantive testing and in evaluating the overall financial statements. As a result, in the overall review stage the expectations developed are not as precise as those developed in performing substantive tests.

Relationship of Analytical Procedures to the Audit Risk Model

2.16 Question 8: How does the auditor's assessment of inherent risk affect the auditor's decision to use analytical procedures and the level of assurance provided by those procedures?

2.17 Answer: The influence of inherent risk on the auditor's decision to use analytical procedures, and the assurance provided from them, is dependent on the extent to which inherent risk affects the precision of the expectation. As noted in question 1, the nature of the account and the environment (factors affecting inherent risk) affect the precision of the expectation. The more susceptible an assertion is to misstatement (absent related internal control) and the less predictable the account, the higher the inherent risk and the less precise an expectation will necessarily be.

2.18 Question 9: How does the assessment of control risk affect an auditor's decision to use analytical procedures and the level of assurance provided by those procedures?

2.19 Answer: The influence of control risk on the auditor's decision to use analytical procedures, and the assurance provided from them, are dependent on the extent to which control risk affects the precision of the expectation. Control risk is directly related to data reliability. In addition, data reliability directly affects expectation precision. Therefore, if financial data produced by the entity are used in developing the expectation and the auditor wishes to form a precise expectation, he or she should take steps to determine that the data used in developing the expectation are reliable. However, this does not preclude the auditor from performing analytical procedures when control risk has not been tested.

2.20 Question 10: When assessing the risks of material misstatement (in other words, the combined assessment of inherent and control risk) in planning a sample for a substantive test of details (statistical or nonstatistical), can the results of analytical procedures be used as a factor in determining the sample size?

2.21 Answer: Yes. As discussed in the AICPA Audit Guide *Audit Sampling*, an auditor assesses the risks of material misstatement and relies on analytical procedures and substantive tests of details in whatever combination he or she believes adequately controls audit risk. If the auditor assesses risks of material misstatement at a lower level, he or she can accept a greater risk of incorrect acceptance for the planned substantive test. As the acceptable level of risk of incorrect acceptance increases, the appropriate sample size for the substantive test decreases. Conversely, if the auditor assesses risks of material misstatement at a higher level, the acceptable level of risk of incorrect acceptance decreases and the appropriate sample size increases. A similar relationship is true for the auditor's reliance on other substantive tests, including analytical procedures related to the same audit objective. As the auditor's reliance on the other related substantive test increases, the acceptable level of risk of incorrect acceptance increases and the appropriate sample size decreases. Conversely, as the auditor's reliance on the other related substantive tests decreases, the acceptable level of risk of incorrect acceptance decreases and the appropriate sample size increases.

Evaluation and Investigation

2.22 Question 11: When does the auditor perform further investigation based upon the findings of an analytical procedure?

2.23 Answer: When a difference between the auditor's expectation and the recorded amount exceeds the amount of difference from the expectation that can be accepted without further explanation, the auditor should identify and consider plausible explanations for the difference. The determining factor to such a consideration is the precision of the expectation. If the auditor concludes that the expectation is so precise that the range of expected differences is sufficiently narrow, the auditor might conclude that the difference between the expectation and the recorded amount represents a misstatement of the account balance. Further analysis involves determining whether all the relevant factors were considered in developing the expectation (that is, was the expectation sufficiently precise to achieve the desired level of assurance). Plausible explanations arising from failing to consider all relevant factors usually relate to unusual transactions or events or to accounting or business changes. If the auditor rules out other plausible, nonmisstatement explanations for the difference, the auditor should then further investigate for misstatement causes.

2.24 In establishing the amount of difference from the expectation that can be accepted without further explanation, the auditor considers not just the magnitude of an individual difference, but also the effect such a difference would have when aggregated with other audit differences.

2.25 Question 12: How does the auditor evaluate differences in excess of the auditor's threshold between the expected and recorded amounts?

2.26 Answer: If the difference between expected and recorded amounts is likely due to potential misstatement, the auditor should perform further analysis and inquiry. (See the "Identification and Investigation" and "Evaluation" sections of chapter 1, "The Use of Analytical Procedures," for situations in which the unexpected difference is not due to a misstatement.) The auditor should obtain sufficient appropriate evidence by performing other audit procedures and inquiring of management about the difference between the expectation formed and the recorded amount. Considering possible explanations for the difference before inquiring of management will likely improve the accuracy of the evaluation of the difference. If a reasonable explanation cannot be obtained, in accordance with paragraph .11 of AU-C section 450, *Evaluation of Misstatements Identified During the Audit* (AICPA, *Professional Standards*), the auditor should determine whether uncorrected misstatements are material, individually or in the aggregate. In making this determination, the auditor should consider (*a*) the size and nature of the misstatements, both in relation to particular classes of transactions, account balances, or disclosures and the financial statements as a whole, and the particular circumstances of their occurrence and (*b*) the effect of uncorrected misstatements related to prior periods on the relevant classes of transactions, account balances, or disclosures and the financial statements as a whole.

Purpose of Analytical Procedures

2.27 Question 13: Can analytical procedures provide evidence about the effectiveness of internal control over financial reporting?

2.28 Answer: As discussed in chapter 1, analytical procedures are performed for three purposes: (*a*) to assist the auditor in planning the nature, timing, and extent of audit procedures;[1] (*b*) to reduce risk in testing account balances; and (*c*) to assess the conclusions reached and evaluate the overall financial statement presentation. However, the result from the analytical procedure and the subsequent evaluation of the unexpected difference can lead the auditor to reevaluate control risk. This is similar to the situation in which the identification of more misstatements than expected from a test of details leads to a reconsideration of the strength of controls.

2.29 Question 14: What are the differences, if any, between substantive analytical procedures performed in an audit, a review, and an attest engagement?

---

[1] In accordance with paragraphs .A7–.A10 of AU-C section 315, *Understanding the Entity and Its Environment and Assessing the Risks of Material Misstatement* (AICPA, *Professional Standards*), analytical procedures may also be performed as risk assessment procedures to obtain an understanding of the entity and its environment. Refer to AU-C section 315 for further guidance.

2.30 Answer: The primary difference in analytical procedures performed in an audit versus a review is the desired level of assurance. In an audit, the substantive analytical procedures performed are designed to provide assurance that the financial statements are fairly presented. In a review, the analytical procedures are performed in connection with inquiries of management to provide limited assurance that the accountant is not aware of any material misstatements. An auditor requires a more precise expectation in an audit than in a review because the audit requires a higher level of assurance.

2.31 This concept also applies when performing analytical procedures in an attest engagement related to financial matters (for example, examination of pro forma financial information). If the accountant performs an examination of management's assertion and performs analytical procedures to provide a high level of assurance, a practitioner requires a more precise expectation than if the practitioner is to provide limited assurance under a review.

2.32 Question 15: What is the role of analytical procedures in planning when the auditor knows from past experience that numerous adjustments are posted to the working trial balance during the engagement?

2.33 Answer: In planning the audit, the auditor should perform analytical procedures that assist in understanding the client's business and material classes of transactions and in determining the nature, timing, and extent of substantive tests. Known or expected adjustments in account balances do not preclude the auditor from performing analytical procedures during planning, and such procedures should be used to assist the auditor in directing attention to potential material misstatements. The auditor should incorporate his or her knowledge of known adjustments in forming more precise expectations.

2.34 Question 16: How does the interrelation among accounts affect the level of assurance provided by the substantive analytical procedures on the individual accounts? For example, does finding that commission expense is 6 percent of sales as expected provide completeness assurance on both sales and commissions?

2.35 Answer: Amounts that are the consequence of other amounts, such as the example cited previously, should be considered carefully when assessing the reliability of data in applying analytical procedures to avoid circular reasoning. The auditor should consider whether the amounts and accounts are independent of one another. In the example noted previously, testing commission expense by comparing the recorded amount with the 6 percent of sales may provide assurance concerning commission expense. However, this same relationship should not be used to predict sales because commission expense is not independent of sales. Therefore, the auditor should not gain assurance from analytical procedures applied to amounts that are not independent of one another.

2.36 Question 17: Is it ever appropriate for an auditor to propose an adjustment based on the results of analytical procedures?

2.37 Answer: In a given situation, an auditor may be able to propose an adjustment for a certain type of account balance. The auditor should consider the level of desired assurance and whether any other substantive tests may assist the auditor in determining a material misstatement. For example, the auditor may consider proposing an adjustment for an unexpected difference found when performing analytical procedures on an estimate, such as a loan loss reserve.

Fraud

2.38 Question 18: How effective are analytical procedures for detecting management fraud?

2.39 Answer: Although analytical procedures would not determine the presence or absence of fraud, they can be an effective means for directing the auditor's attention to the possible existence of management fraud. In most cases, the effectiveness of the analytical procedures are enhanced if the auditor uses industry knowledge, knowledge of relations among financial and nonfinancial data, and data from reliable sources.

2.40 Paragraphs .22 and .34 of AU-C section 240, *Consideration of Fraud in a Financial Statement Audit* (AICPA, *Professional Standards*), discuss the use of analytical procedures in the risk assessment process to help identify risks of material misstatement due to fraud.

> **.22** Based on analytical procedures performed as part of risk assessment procedures, the auditor should evaluate whether unusual or unexpected relationships that have been identified indicate risks of material misstatement due to fraud. To the extent not already included, the analytical procedures, and evaluation thereof, should include procedures relating to revenue accounts.
>
> **.34** The auditor should evaluate, at or near the end of the audit, whether the accumulated results of auditing procedures (including analytical procedures that were performed as substantive tests or when forming an overall conclusion) affect the assessment of the risks of material misstatement due to fraud made earlier in the audit or indicate a previously unrecognized risk of material misstatement due to fraud. If not already performed when forming an overall conclusion, the analytical procedures relating to revenue, required by paragraph .22, should be performed through the end of the reporting period.

2.41 Paragraph .01 of AU section 316, *Consideration of Fraud in a Financial Statement Audit* (AICPA, *PCAOB Standards and Related Rules*, Interim Standards), states that when performing an integrated audit of financial statements and internal control over financial reporting, refer to paragraphs 14–15 of PCAOB Auditing Standard No. 5, *An Audit of Internal Control Over Financial Reporting That Is Integrated with An Audit of Financial Statements* (AICPA, *PCAOB Standards and Related Rules*, Auditing Standards), regarding fraud considerations, in addition to the fraud considerations set forth in AU section 316.

Chapter 3

Case Study: On the Go Stores

©Update 3-1 *Audit*: Clarified Auditing Standards

The auditing guidance in this guide edition has been conformed to Statement on Auditing Standards (SAS) Nos. 122–125, which were issued in 2011 as part of the Auditing Standards Board's Clarity Project. These clarified SASs are effective for periods ending on or after December 15, 2012. Early application is not permitted. Although extensive, the revisions to generally accepted auditing standards resulting from these clarified SASs do not change many of the requirements found in the auditing standards that they supersede.

To assist auditors and financial reporting professionals in making the transition, this guide includes appendix C, "Mapping and Summarization of Changes—Clarified Auditing Standards," which provides a cross reference of the sections in the superseded auditing standards to the applicable sections in the clarified auditing standards and identifies the changes, either substantive or primarily clarifying in nature, that may affect an auditor's practice or methodology relative to the applicable sections of SAS Nos. 122–125. It also summarizes the changes resulting from the requirements of SAS Nos. 122–125.

The preface of this guide and the Financial Reporting Center on www.aicpa.org provide more information on the Clarity Project. Visit www.aicpa.org/sasclarity.

3.01 This chapter provides a case study for On the Go Stores. The case study illustrates the four types of expectation methods discussed in chapter 1, "The Use of Analytical Procedures," of this guide: trend analysis, ratio analysis, reasonableness testing, and regression analysis.

3.02 This case illustrates the use of analytical procedures in both planning and substantive testing for current year sales for a chain of convenience stores named On the Go Stores. The case illustrates the use and effectiveness of the different types of analytical procedures and the factors affecting the precision of each. For example, there are illustrations for trend analysis, ratio analysis, reasonableness testing, and regression analysis in which the analytical procedures are based on financial and nonfinancial data.

Background Information

3.03 On the Go Stores has 23 convenience stores located in the Southeast. Included in the 23 stores are 5 new stores (nos. 1, 4, 10, 13, and 22) that opened during the year. Operations vary by geographic location and the mix of products sold.

3.04 The location of a store is based on several factors, such as competition and the economic environment of the location. Store nos. 2, 4, 6, 8, 9, 11, 13, 15, 17, 18, 20, 21, and 23 are considered to be in favorable locations.

3.05 Typically, a store's operations do not change much unless a new product line is introduced, such as selling gas, offering check-cashing services, or selling lottery tickets. The mix of products and services can vary, and the most important factor is whether the store sells gasoline. (Store nos. 5, 6, 7, 8,

14, 15, 16, 17, 18, 19, 20, and 21 sell gasoline.) These additional product lines typically affect the volume of customers as well as the number of full-time employees.

3.06 On the Go Stores provides the information shown in exhibit 3-1.

Exhibit 3-1

Relevant Information for On the Go Stores

Store	*Prior-Year Sales (Audited) ($)*	*Current-Year Sales ($)*	*Dollar Change ($)*	*Current-Percent Change (%)*	*Current-Year Inventory ($)*	*Square Feet*	*Average Number Full-Time Employees*
1*	N/A	781,793	781,793	N/A	48,725	2,500	11.00
2	1,165,221	1,146,438	(18,783)	(1.16)	44,171	2,500	11.31
3	1,147,430	1,195,004	47,574	4.15	45,714	2,500	12.46
4*	N/A	951,784	951,784	N/A	37,218	4,000	11.86
5	2,037,463	1,981,409	(56,054)	(2.75)	45,826	4,000	10.06
6	2,257,920	2,300,671	42,751	1.89	53,862	4,000	11.10
7	1,850,354	1,956,481	106,127	5.74	49,883	4,000	10.71
8	1,916,884	1,799,713	(117,171)	(6.11)	47,016	4,000	7.50
9	1,833,209	1,820,641	(12,568)	(.69)	59,726	4,000	14.00
10*	N/A	774,954	774,954	N/A	35,882	2,500	11.20
11	980,484	1,159,004	178,520	18.21	37,664	2,500	11.60
12	1,069,652	1,139,475	69,823	6.53	34,662	2,500	12.70
13*	N/A	948,522	948,522	N/A	44,782	4,000	11.86
14	1,795,123	1,984,777	189,654	10.56	38,774	4,000	12.20
15	2,119,015	2,293,847	174,832	8.25	55,423	4,000	11.10
16	1,947,303	1,984,722	37,419	1.92	52,884	4,000	10.40
17	1,705,789	1,798,336	92,547	5.43	46,834	4,000	8.84
18	2,396,971	2,484,503	87,532	3.65	53,772	4,000	12.10
19	1,901,631	1,837,400	(64,231)	(3.38)	43,982	4,000	9.70
20	1,514,798	1,609,385	94,587	6.24	44,893	4,000	7.20
21	1,886,587	1,874,229	(12,358)	(.66)	37,665	4,000	10.50
22*	N/A	698,333	698,333	N/A	33,826	2,500	10.50
23	1,092,908	1,198,229	105,321	9.64	44,857	2,500	10.90
Total	30,618,742	35,719,650	5,100,908	16.66	1,038,041	80,000	250.80

* Store opened during current year.

3.07 As discussed in chapter 1, the use of analytical procedures is a process that has four phases, the first being the formation of an expectation. Some of the factors that affect the precision of the expectation are the nature of the account, the assertion, and the environment. The auditor can assume that these factors are constant throughout the examples presented in the case study when forming an expectation.

Nature of the Account or Assertion

3.08

Account: Sales

Assertion: Occurrence or existence of revenue

Audit objective: Overstatement of revenue

Predictability of the relationship: Some examples of factors that the auditor might use to predict sales (predictors) include the following:

- Stable environmental factors (that is, no major changes in employment opportunities or construction activities in the area)
- Prior-year sales
- Product mix (that is, lottery and check cashing)
- Store square feet
- Location (favorable or not favorable)
- Average monthly utility cost per store
- Total labor hours per store
- Inventory turnover rate
- Stores open 24 hours
- Number of employees per store
- The account not affected by management's discretion
- Income statement account

3.09 Factors to be identified and considered that could affect the amount being audited include the following:

- No significant events or accounting changes, except for the opening of the new stores
- Industry and economic factors along with management incentives remaining the same
- Repeat audit engagement
- Materiality $150,000 or 8 percent change from prior year

3.10 All predictors are not considered in any one example; however, as the precision of the expectation increases, more predictors are used. Example 1 (trend analysis) uses only one predictor, prior-year sales, and more predictors are introduced in examples 2–4 (ratio analysis, reasonableness testing, and regression analysis).

Example 1: Trend Analysis

3.11 Trend analysis can be used in the planning phase of an audit or as a substantive test. Trend analysis typically is more appropriate for the planning phase of an audit, because it does not take into consideration changes in specific factors that affect the account. However, considering factors that increase the precision of trend analysis may provide the auditor with an appropriate level of assurance for substantive testing.

Expectation Formation (Phase I)

3.12 Following are the relevant factors that affect the precision of the expectation.

Nature of the Account or Assertion

3.13 This information is provided in the "Background Information" section.

Characteristics of the Data

3.14 Level of detail is as follows:

- Sales data are available for the current and prior year, aggregated by stores open all year and those open part of the year, and disaggregated by store.
- For the planning phase of an audit, aggregated data may be appropriate.
- For substantive testing, disaggregated data by category of store (open all year versus part of the year) may be appropriate when there is a stable environment and reasonable controls are in place.

3.15 Reliability of data is as follows:

- The management of On the Go Stores has provided the current-year sales information.
- Current year sales is unaudited; prior-year sales is audited.

Inherent Precision of the Type of Expectation

3.16 With simple trend analysis, the auditor has the expectation that there will be no change from prior-year sales in the current year (predictor is prior-year sales; when prior-year numbers are used as the predictor, the auditor should consider the precision of the expectation and the potential that he or she is ignoring other changes that may have an effect).

Trend Analysis: Planning Phase of the Audit and Substantive Testing

3.17 When using trend analysis for the planning phase, the use of data aggregated at a high level may be appropriate because a high level of assurance is not expected from the procedure.

	Current Year	*Prior Year*	*Change*	*% Change*
Total sales	$35,719,650	$30,618,742	$5,100,908	16.66%

3.18 Because a higher level of assurance is desired when using analytical procedures as substantive tests, an expectation with greater precision should be formed. This can be done by using disaggregated data, such as sales by store, product mix, and location.

3.19 Sales for the new stores opened during the year equal $4,155,386 (no new stores were opened in the prior year). If that amount were eliminated from the total of current-year sales, the adjusted amount of current-year sales would be $31,564,264, which could be compared to the prior-year amount resulting in a change of $945,522, or 3.09 percent.

Planning Phase: Identification, Investigation, and Evaluation (Phases II–IV)

Identification

3.20 Identification begins with the auditor comparing the expected amount with the recorded amount. Unexpected differences, if any, are compared to the established amount of difference from the expectation that the auditor can accept without further explanation. Because the difference for On the Go Stores in the planning phase is in excess of the threshold of $150,000, or an 8 percent change from prior year, the auditor should design procedures to evaluate the causes of such differences. The auditor could better investigate the difference by disaggregating the data by stores open all year versus stores open part of the year. The auditor should consider whether the 3.09 percent difference is acceptable for the stores open all year.

3.21 Planning is not a discrete phase of the audit, but rather an iterative process that begins with engagement acceptance and continues throughout the audit as the auditor performs audit procedures and accumulates sufficient appropriate audit evidence to support the audit opinion. As a result of performing planned audit procedures, the auditor may obtain disconfirming evidence that might cause the auditor to revise the overall audit strategy. In accordance with AU-C sections 315, *Understanding the Entity and Its Environment and Assessing the Risks of Material Misstatement*, and 520, *Analytical Procedures* (AICPA, *Professional Standards*), the purpose of using analytical procedures in the planning phase of the audit is to obtain an understanding of the entity and its environment to assess the risks of material misstatement, and to design the nature, timing, and extent of auditing procedures. In evaluating the stores open all year, the auditor evaluates whether the results suggest an increased risk in the sales account. If so, the auditor should consider altering the nature, timing, and extent for the substantive tests planned for the audit.

3.22 Trend analysis as a substantive test will be performed on stores that have been open all of the year. The expectation of current year sales by store is the prior-year sales by store.

Substantive Testing: Identification, Investigation, and Evaluation (Phases II–IV)

Identification

3.23 Identification begins by comparing the expected amount with the recorded amount. In this case the analytical procedure is the percentage change from the prior-year to current-year sales as shown in column 5 of exhibit 3-1. The differences are compared with the amount of difference from the expectation that the auditor can accept without further explanation to determine if they are unexpected. In this case, the auditor uses a threshold of an 8 percent change when determining if differences identified should be investigated. Therefore, the procedure identifies store nos. 11, 14, 15, and 23 for further investigation.

Investigation

3.24 As stated in chapter 1, unexpected differences can be due to misstatements or to factors not considered in the development of the expectation. If the auditor believes the unexpected difference could be caused by factors not considered in the development of the expectation (for example, differences in stores that sell gas or lottery tickets), the auditor might consider whether developing a more precise expectation can be cost-effective, such as disaggregated information by product line within a store or adjusting the analysis for general inflation. Otherwise the auditor should consider what additional substantive procedures should be performed. Paragraph .07 of AU-C section 520 states that inquiry of management may assist the auditor in determining the causes of the unexpected differences. However, management responses should be corroborated with other audit evidence. For example, if management explains the increase in current-year sales as a result of a new product line that was introduced only in the current year, the auditor could perform a sales analysis to determine that the items were sold only in the current year and did not appear in the prior-year sales analysis.

Evaluation

3.25 The results from a second, more precise trend analysis or additional substantive testing to verify the explanations provided by management may provide the auditor with a basis of concluding whether a material misstatement exists. Paragraph .07 of AU-C section 450, *Evaluation of Misstatements Identified During the Audit* (AICPA, *Professional Standards*), states that the auditor should communicate on a timely basis and request management to record the adjustment needed to correct all known misstatements, including the effect of prior period misstatements (see paragraph .11 of AU-C section 450), other than those that the auditor believes are trivial.

Example 2: Ratio Analysis

3.26 A ratio analysis involves the comparison of relationships between financial statement accounts, a comparison of an account with nonfinancial data, or a comparison of relationships across an industry, such as gross profit comparisons. See appendix B, "Financial Ratios," of this guide for additional helpful ratios.

Expectation Formation (Phase I)

3.27 These are the relevant factors that affect the precision of the expectation.

Nature of the Account or Assertion

3.28 The "Background Information" section contains this information.

Characteristics of the Data

3.29 Level of detail is as follows:

- The auditor has available sales data and cost of goods sold data for stores open all year that sell gas and that do not sell gas.

3.30 Reliability of data is as follows:

- The management of On the Go Stores has provided the auditor with total sales and cost of goods sold data for stores open all year by those that sell gas and those that do not sell gas.
- Sales and cost of goods sold information are unaudited; however, the gross margin percentage can be calculated by the auditor to ensure mathematical accuracy.

Inherent Precision of the Type of Expectation

3.31 *Ratio analysis.* The predictor is the gross profit percentage for stores that sell gas compared with stores that do not sell gas. A higher gross profit percentage is expected for stores that sell gas due to higher volume.

	Current Year	*Prior Year*
All stores open all year (excludes new stores):		
Total sales	$31,564,264	$30,618,742
Cost of goods sold	21,463,700	21,987,932
Gross margin	$10,100,564	$8,630,810
Gross margin percentage	31.99%	28.19%
Stores that sell gas:		
Total sales	$23,905,473	$23,329,838
Cost of goods sold	16,112,291	16,307,557
Gross margin	$7,793,182	$7,022,281
Gross margin percentage	32.6%	30.1%
Stores that do not sell gas:		
Total sales	$7,658,791	$7,288,904
Cost of goods sold	5,351,409	5,680,375
Gross margin	$2,307,382	$1,608,529
Gross margin percentage	30.1%	22.1%

Identification, Investigation, and Evaluation (Phases II–IV)

Identification

3.32 Identification begins by comparing the expected amount with the recorded amount. In this case the analytical procedure is the comparison of the gross profit percentage for the current to prior year for stores that sell gas and stores that do not sell gas. The differences are compared with the amount of difference from the expectation that the auditor can accept without further explanation to determine if they are unexpected. For example, assume that an acceptable difference for a certain On the Go Store is 10 percent. The percentage threshold will not necessarily be the same for trend and ratio analysis. The auditor should use professional judgment to determine the threshold based on materiality, risk, and the objective of the procedure. Using the aggregate analysis for all stores open all year, the procedure identifies an unexpected difference of 13.5 percent in gross margin percentage (31.99 percent – 28.19 percent / 28.19 percent). However, a more precise expectation can better identify the source of the unexpected difference. Specifically, for the stores that sell gas, the difference in gross margin percentage is only 8.3 percent (32.6 percent – 30.1 percent / 30.1 percent) which is below the threshold. In contrast, the difference in gross margin percentage for those stores that do not sell gas is 36.5 percent (30.1 percent – 22.1 percent / 22.1 percent). This suggests that the 6 stores that do not sell gas should be investigated further.

Investigation

3.33 If the auditor believes the unexpected difference could be caused by other factors not considered in the development of the expectation (for example, location or degree of competition), the auditor might consider whether developing a more precise expectation can be cost-effective. Otherwise the auditor should consider what additional substantive procedures should be performed. Paragraph .07 of AU-C section 520 states that inquiry of management may assist the auditor in determining the causes of the unexpected differences. However, management responses should be corroborated with other audit evidence.

Evaluation

3.34 The results from a second, more precise reasonableness test or additional substantive testing on the stores that do not sell gas may provide the auditor with a basis of concluding whether a material misstatement exists. Paragraph .07 of AU-C section 450 states that the auditor should communicate on a timely basis and request management to record the adjustment needed to correct all known misstatements, including the effect of prior period misstatements (see paragraph .11 of AU-C section 450), other than those that the auditor believes are trivial.

3.35 This example shows how the use of financial ratios, along with disaggregated information, can increase the precision of the expectation.

Example 3: Reasonableness Test

3.36 A reasonableness test is an analysis of an account balance that involves developing an expectation based on financial data, nonfinancial data, or both.

Expectation Formation (Phase I)

3.37 Following are the relevant factors that affect the precision of the expectation.

Nature of the Account or Assertion

3.38 This information is provided in the "Background Information" section.

Characteristics of the Data

3.39 Level of detail is as follows:

- The auditor has available sales data and square footage data by store.

3.40 Reliability of data is as follows:

- The management of On the Go Stores has provided the auditor with the amount of square footage per store and sales per stores (see exhibit 3-1). The region's average sales per square footage can be obtained from information provided by the National Association of

Convenience Stores (NACS), which publishes information on the convenience store industry.

- Sales information is unaudited; however, square footage data can be independently verified by the auditor to increase its reliability.

Inherent Precision of the Type of Expectation

3.41 *Reasonableness test.* The predictor is sales per square foot by store.

3.42 In performing a reasonableness test of On the Go Stores' current-year sales using the information provided, the auditor calculates the average sales amount per square foot and compares it with the region's average sales per square foot. If only a low level of assurance is desired from the procedure, conducting the test using aggregated data is appropriate. However, a higher level of assurance may be obtained through the formation of a more precise expectation, for example, by disaggregation by store as shown in exhibit 3-2.

Exhibit 3-2

Reasonableness Test Based on Sales per Square Foot

Store	*Current Year Sales* ($)	*Square Feet*	*Sales per Square Foot* ($)	*Average per Square Foot per NACS* ($)	*Difference* ($)	*Difference* (%)
1*	781,793	2,500	313	490	177	36.20
2	1,146,438	2,500	459	490	31	6.40
3	1,195,004	2,500	478	490	12	2.40
4*	951,784	4,000	238	490	252	51.40
5	1,981,409	4,000	495	490	(5)	(1.10)
6	2,300,671	4,000	575	490	(85)	(17.40)
7	1,956,481	4,000	489	490	1	.02
8	1,799,713	4,000	450	490	40	8.20
9	1,820,641	4,000	455	490	35	7.10
10*	774,954	2,500	310	490	180	36.70
11	1,159,004	2,500	464	490	26	5.40
12	1,139,475	2,500	456	490	34	7.00
13*	948,522	4,000	237	490	253	51.60
14	1,984,777	4,000	496	490	(6)	(1.30)
15	2,293,847	4,000	573	490	(83)	(17.00)
16	1,984,722	4,000	496	490	(6)	(1.30)
17	1,798,336	4,000	450	490	40	8.20
18	2,484,503	4,000	621	490	(131)	(26.80)
19	1,837,400	4,000	459	490	31	6.30
20	1,609,385	4,000	402	490	88	17.90
21	1,874,229	4,000	469	490	21	4.40
22*	698,333	2,500	279	490	211	43.00
23	1,198,229	2,500	479	490	11	2.20
Total	35,719,650	80,000	446	490	—	—

* Store opened during current year.

3.43 After reviewing the information provided by NACS, the auditor determines that the information reflects only stores that have been in operation for a full year; therefore, it would be appropriate to isolate the stores that have been open for less than a full year, as in the following table:

Reasonableness Testing—Total for Stores Open All Year

	Sales	*Total Square Footage*
Total sales and square footage for the year	$35,719,650	80,000
Less: sales and square footage for stores opened part of the year (store nos. 1, 4, 10, 13, 22)	4,155,386	15,500
Sales and square footage for stores opened for full year	$31,564,264	64,500
Average sales per square foot (provided by NACS)		x $490
Expected total sales for stores open for a full year		$31,605,000
Actual On the Go sales for the current year (stores open for a full year)		31,564,264
Difference		$40,736 or 0.13%

3.44 To perform reasonableness testing by store, the auditor calculates the sales per square foot for each store and ranks the results (see exhibit 3-2). The results for the 5 new stores are relatively small and can be disregarded for this analysis. The remaining stores can be compared to the $490 national average square foot, provided by NACS.

Identification, Investigation, and Evaluation (Phases II–IV)

Identification

3.45 The auditor begins identification by comparing the expected amount with the recorded amount. In this case the analytical procedure is the difference from the NACS average sales per square foot to recorded current year sales per square foot, as calculated in exhibit 3-2. The differences are compared with the amount of difference from the expectation that the auditor can accept without further explanation to determine if they are unexpected. For example, the threshold is 15 percent, and any changes greater than the threshold are considered an unexpected difference and investigated. According to the aggregate analysis for the stores open all year, the results do not identify an unusual fluctuation based on the materiality threshold. However, the analysis by store for the stores open all year identifies store nos. 6, 15, 18, and 20 for further investigation.

Investigation

3.46 If the auditor accepts the difference of 0.13 percent calculated in the first reasonableness test, the sales account balance is accepted without further investigation. However, the second reasonableness test, which is more precise because it is based on disaggregated data, does indicate the need for further investigation. If the auditor believes the unexpected difference could be caused by factors not considered in the development of the expectation (for example, differences in stores that sell gas or operate in more favorable locations), the auditor might consider whether developing a more precise expectation can be cost-effective. Otherwise the auditor should consider what additional substantive procedures should be performed. Paragraph .07 of AU-C section 520 states that inquiry of management may assist the auditor in determining the causes of the unexpected differences. However, management responses should be corroborated with other audit evidence.

Evaluation

3.47 If the auditor accepts the results of the first reasonableness test as sufficient appropriate evidence for the existence of sales, no evaluation is performed. However, this test is relatively imprecise and is applicable only if the auditor desires a low level of assurance. The results of the second, more precise reasonableness test followed by additional investigation may provide the auditor with a basis of concluding whether a material misstatement exists. Paragraph .07 of AU-C section 450 states that the auditor should communicate on a timely basis and request management to record the adjustment needed to correct all known misstatements, including the effect of prior period misstatements (see paragraph .11 of AU-C section 450), other than those that the auditor believes are trivial.

3.48 This example illustrates how the use of financial and independent nonfinancial information can give the auditor a greater precision in forming the expectation and in return provide a greater level of assurance.

Example 4: Regression Analysis

3.49 Regression analysis has the same objective as trend, ratio analysis, and reasonableness testing, that is, to identify the potential for misstatement. The advantage of regression analysis over the other methods is that the regression: (*a*) provides an explicit, mathematically objective, and precise method for forming an expectation; (*b*) allows the inclusion of a larger number of relevant independent variables; and (*c*) provides direct and quantitative measures of the precision of the expectation.

3.50 The auditor's specific objective in using regression for On the Go Stores is to determine which store should be targeted for initial investigation for potential misstatement in sales. The regression analysis determines which stores have total sales that are most out of line in comparison with the others. This type of analysis is called cross-sectional regression (as opposed to longitudinal or time-series regression) because a cross-section of relevant information about each store is used in determining which stores are most unusual. In predicting sales, the cross-sectional data usually include relevant predictors, such as the size of the store (as used in the reasonableness testing preceding), and other features that cause higher sales at the store, such as whether it sells gas, sells lottery tickets, and so on.

3.51 The alternative type of regression is called time-series regression because it uses the data from several (usually 20–40) prior audited (usually monthly) time periods to develop a regression model to predict future periods. A time-series model is used to predict the monthly sales figures for the current audit year based on prior year data in order to assess the reasonableness of the reported monthly sales figures. Both types of regression analysis can be used to provide substantive appropriate evidence. The type of regression used in the following example is cross-sectional.

Cross-Sectional Regression

3.52 The auditor begins a regression application for On the Go Stores by selecting the dependent variable, in this case, the amount of sales (includes merchandise sales and gas sales) at each of the 23 stores. The audit objective is to examine sales analytically to determine the potential for overstatement and to address the auditor's objectives for testing occurrence and existence. A preliminary assessment of materiality is set at $150,000. Second, the auditor selects the relevant independent variables, that is, those factors that the auditor knows from experience with the client and industry will be useful predictors of sales at each store.

Independent Variables

3.53 The independent variables are as follows (see exhibit 3-3 for data):

- The level of inventory (merchandise plus gas) at the store.
- The number of staff at the store (full-time equivalent employees, or FTEs).
- Whether the store opened or closed during the year, or for any reason was not open the entire year. This variable is entered as a binary, or "0/1" variable: a 0 if the store was open all year, and a 1 if the store was open only part of the year.
- Distinctive characteristics of each store, such as whether it sells gas. This variable is also entered as a binary variable: a value of 1 if it sells gas, and a value of 0 if it does not sell gas.
- Square feet of floor space at each store. In this case, there are only 2 size stores (1 at 2,500 square feet and 1 at 4,000 square feet). Thus, for simplicity and clarity this variable is entered into the regression as a binary variable, which has a value of 0 for stores with 2,500 square feet, and a value of 1 for stores of 4,000 square feet.

3.54 Depending on the auditor's local knowledge, additional variables might be included, for example, whether the store has a check-cashing facility, whether it is an attractive location (for example, near to an intersection of highways, a ballpark, or other "draw" of customers), the number of parking places, and other factors about the general competitive environment for the store.

Exhibit 3-3

Regression Variables for On the Go Stores

Store	*Merchandise Inventory ($)*	*Full-Time Employees*	*New Store*	*Sells Gas*	*Size*	*Sales ($)*
1	48,725	11.00	1	0	0	781,793
2	44,171	11.31	0	0	0	1,146,438
3	45,714	12.46	0	0	0	1,195,004
4	37,218	11.86	1	0	1	951,784
5	45,826	10.06	0	1	1	1,981,409
6	53,862	11.10	0	1	1	2,300,671
7	49,883	10.71	0	1	1	1,956,481
8	47,016	7.50	0	1	1	1,799,713
9	59,726	14.00	0	0	1	1,820,641
10	35,882	11.20	1	0	0	774,954
11	37,664	11.60	0	0	0	1,159,004
12	34,662	12.70	0	0	0	1,139,475
13	44,782	11.86	1	0	1	948,522
14	38,774	12.20	0	1	1	1,984,777
15	55,423	11.10	0	1	1	2,293,847
16	52,884	10.40	0	1	1	1,984,722
17	46,834	8.84	0	1	1	1,798,336
18	53,772	12.10	0	1	1	2,484,503
19	43,982	9.70	0	1	1	1,837,400
20	44,893	7.20	0	1	1	1,609,385
21	37,665	10.50	0	1	1	1,874,229
22	33,826	10.50	1	0	0	698,333
23	44,857	10.90	0	0	0	1,198,229

3.55 The auditor enters the data into an Excel spreadsheet (other spreadsheet programs and statistical systems can also be used) and performs a regression analysis on the data. In Excel, this is accomplished through the following five steps:

1. From the File Tab, choose Options (see exhibit 3-4).

Exhibit 3-4

Selecting Excel Options

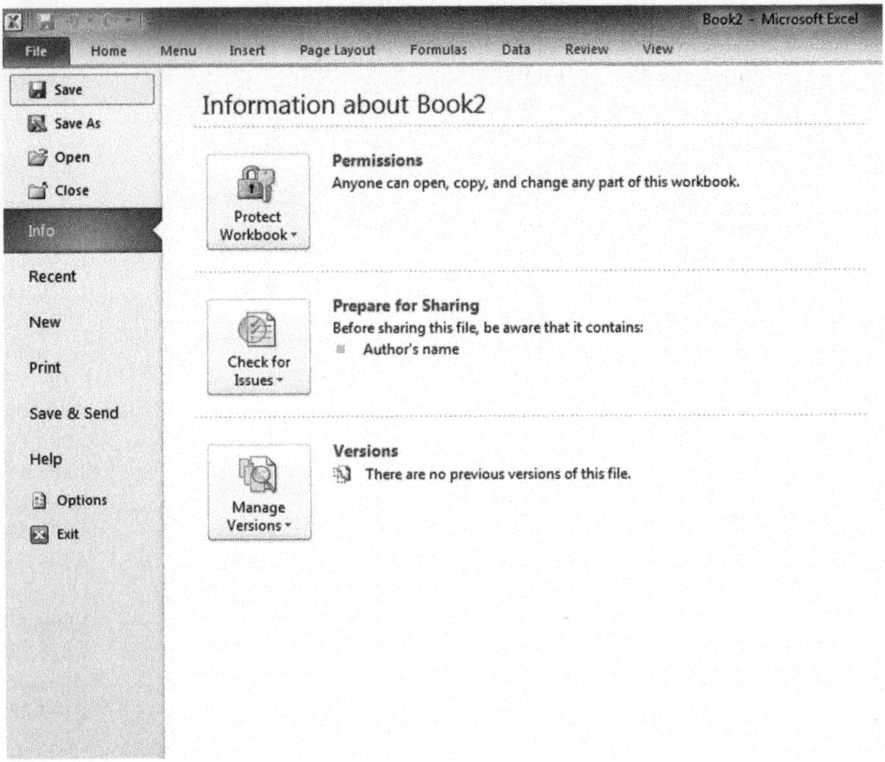

2. From the Options menu, select Add-Ins, then use the drop-down box at the bottom of the page to Manage: Excel Add-ins, and select Go (see exhibit 3-5).

Exhibit 3-5

Selecting Excel Add-Ins

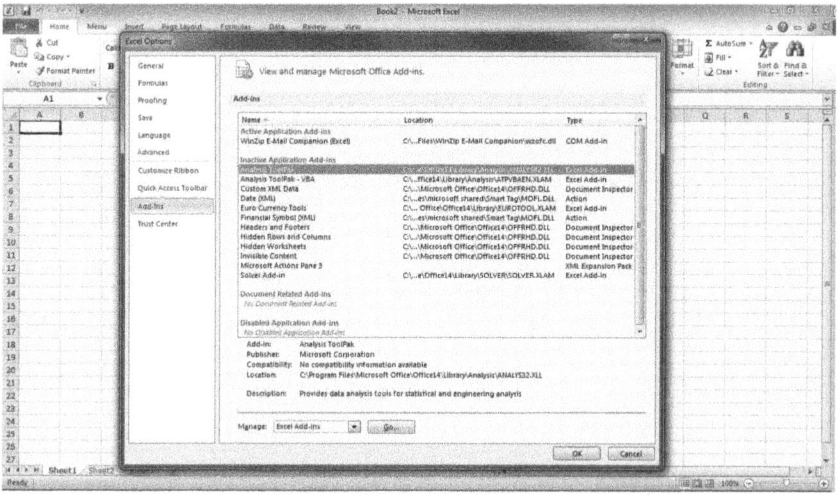

3. From the Excel Add-Ins Page, select Analysis ToolPak, and select OK (see exhibit 3-6).

Exhibit 3-6

Selecting Analysis Tool Pak to Install Regression

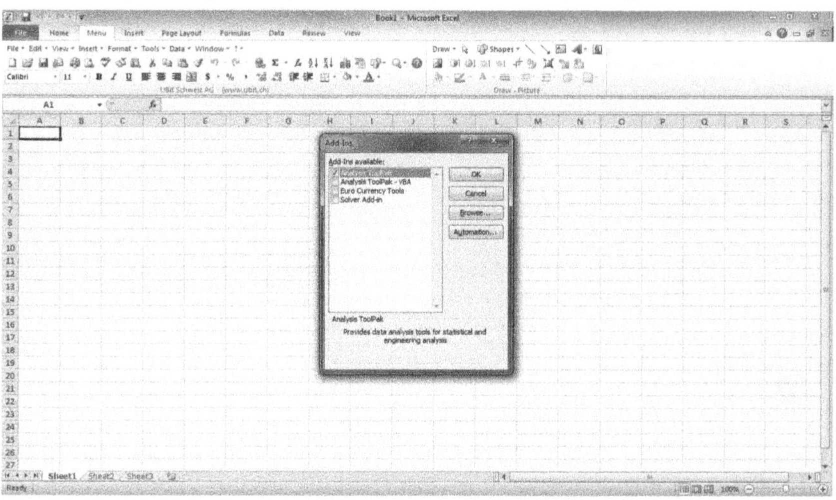

3.56 The effect of these first three steps is to install regression (and other statistical procedures) so they are available in Excel. (Please note that the version of Excel used in the case study is Office 2010. Upgraded versions may be available.)

4. Select the Data Tab, and select Data Analysis and choose Regression from the Data Analysis box, then select OK (see exhibit 3-7).

Exhibit 3-7

Selecting Regression in Excel

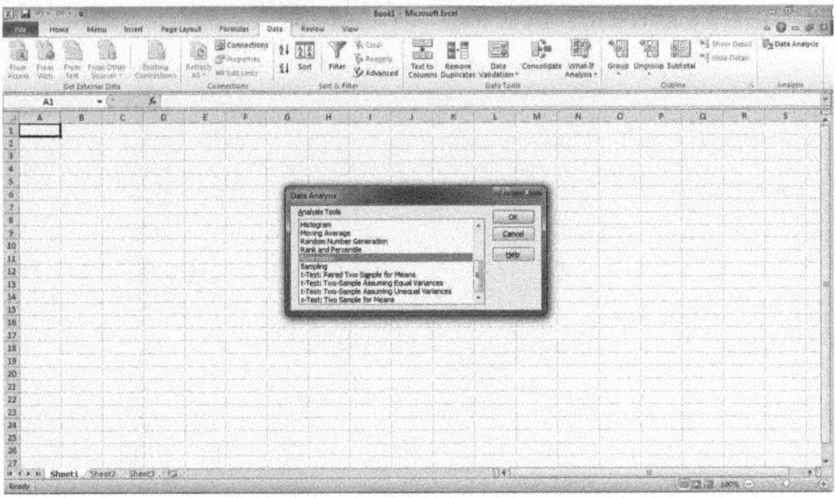

5. Complete 3 items in the Regression box (see exhibit 3-8).

Exhibit 3-8

Entering the Necessary Information Into the Excel Regression Procedure

a. Enter the spreadsheet ranges of the dependent and independent variables (the variables are entered in columns, a row for each store. In this case, G7:G30 and B7:F30 are the ranges for the dependent and independent variables respectively; also, include in these ranges a row at the top which gives the name of the variable in each column so the regression output will label the variables properly).

b. Select Labels.

c. Select the location for the output among the report options (in this case, the cell A40).

d. To calculate the residual amounts for each item, select the Residual's box in exhibit 3-8.

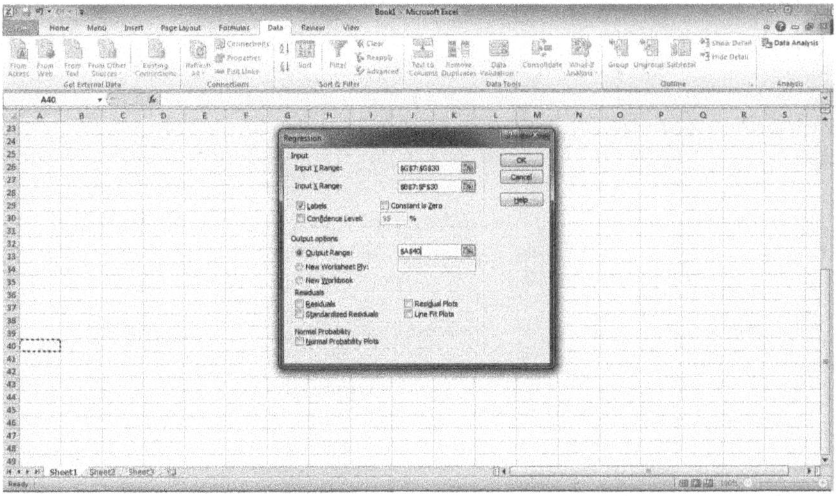

3.57 The regression results for On the Go Stores are shown in exhibits 3-9 and 3-10.

Exhibit 3-9

Regression Results for All Variables

SUMMARY OUTPUT
Regression Statistics

(*Note:* The important information in the Summary Output Table is the R squared value, .975, and the standard error, $97,961.)

SUMMARY OUTPUT

Regression Statistics	
Multiple R	0.987
R Squared	0.975
Adjusted R Squared	0.967
Standard Error	97,961
Observations	23

ANOVA

	df	*SS*	*MS*	*F*	*Significance F*
Regression	5	6.314E+12	1.263E+12	1.316E+02	5.680E-13
Residual	17	1.631E+11			
Total	22	6.478E+12			

	Coefficients	*Standard Error*	*t Stat*	*P-Value*	*Lower 95%*	*Upper 95%*
Intercept	(746,293)	244,813	(3.048)	0.007	(1,262,804)	(229,783)
Inventory	16.1179	4	4.504	0.000	9	24

(continued)

	Coefficients	*Standard Error*	*t Stat*	*P-Value*	*Lower 95%*	*Upper 95%*
FTE	106,114	17,725	5.987	0.000	68,717	143,511
New Store	(303,431)	67,863	(4.471)	0.000	(446,609)	(160,253)
Sells Gas	804,866	94,751	8.495	0.000	604,959	1,004,773
Size-Loc	93,247	77,838	1.198	0.247	(70,977)	257,470

RESIDUAL OUTPUT (*Note:* A negative number means potential understatement; a positive number means potential overstatement.)

Observation	*Predicted Sales*	*Residuals*
1	902,875	(121,082)
2	1,165,801	(19,363)
3	1,312,702	(117,698)
4	901,911	49,873
5	1,957,946	23,463
6	2,197,829	102,842
7	2,092,311	(135,830)
8	1,705,475	94,238
9	1,795,209	25,432
10	717,095	57,859
11	1,091,694	67,310
12	1,160,034	(20,559)
13	1,023,827	(75,305)
14	2,071,367	(86,590)
15	2,222,989	70,858
16	2,107,786	(123,064)
17	1,844,734	(46,398)
18	2,302,492	182,011
19	1,890,024	(52,624)
20	1,639,423	(30,038)
21	1,873,098	1,131
22	609,677	88,656
23	1,133,351	64,878

Exhibit 3-10

Regression Results for On the Go Stores With the Size Variable Removed

SUMMARY OUTPUT

Regression Statistics	
Multiple R	0.986
R Squared	0.973
Adjusted R Squared	0.967
Standard Error	99,138
Observations	23

ANOVA

	df	*SS*	*MS*	*F*	*Significance F*
Regression	4	6.30072E+12	1.575E+12	160.26934	8.2455E-14
Residual	18	1.7691E+11	9.828E+09		
Total	22	6.47763E+12			

	Coefficients	*Standard Error*	*t Stat*	*P-Value*	*Lower 95%*	*Upper 95%*
Intercept	(865,347)	226,422	-3.822	0.001	(1,341,043)	(389,651)
Inventory	17.5503	3	5.141	0.000	10	25
FTE	111,944	17,249	6.490	0.000	75,705	148,183
New Store	(270,284)	62,710	-4.310	0.000	(402,034)	(138,535)
Sells Gas	890,046	63,378	14.043	0.000	756,894	1,023,198

RESIDUAL OUTPUT (*Note:* A negative number means potential understatement; a positive number means potential overstatement.)

Observation	*Predicted Sales*	*Residuals*
1	950,891	(169,098)
2	1,175,955	(29,517)
3	1,331,770	(136,766)
4	845,212	106,572
5	1,955,116	26,293
6	2,212,572	88,099
7	2,099,081	(142,600)
8	1,689,424	110,289
9	1,750,079	70,562
10	747,882	27,072
11	1,094,219	64,785
12	1,164,671	(25,196)
13	977,963	(29,441)
14	2,070,912	(86,135)
15	2,239,968	53,879
16	2,117,047	(132,325)

(continued)

Observation	Predicted Sales	Residuals
17	1,836,235	(37,899)
18	2,322,937	161,566
19	1,882,454	(45,054)
20	1,618,582	(9,197)
21	1,861,144	13,085
22	633,438	64,895
23	1,142,097	56,132

3.58 The assessment of the precision of the regression involves a consideration of the R squared, t statistic, and standard error of the estimate, which are contained in the "Summary Output" section of the spreadsheet report. The proper interpretation of these three values is explained in appendix A, "Measures of Precision for a Regression Analysis," of this guide.

Expectation Formation (Phase I)

3.59 When using regression, expectation formation is accomplished by the regression analysis, using the independent variables entered by the auditor, as shown in the "Coefficients" column of exhibit 3-9. For On the Go Stores, the expectation model is the following regression model:

Sales = – $746,293 + 16.1179 x inventory
+ $106,114 x full-time employees
– $303,431 x new store
+ $804,866 x sells gas
+ $93,247 x size

3.60 For example, the expectation for sales in store no. 2 is derived by using the equation in the following way (data from exhibit 3-3):

Sales = – $746,293 + 16.1179 x $44,171
+ $106,114 x 11.31
– $303,431 x 0
+ $804,866 x 0
+ $93,247 x 0
= $1,165,800

3.61 The regression prediction for sales can be compared to the actual value of sales for store no. 2, $1,146,438. The difference, $19,362 ($1,165,800 – $1,146,438), is a measure of the degree to which store no. 2 differs from the other stores, based on a regression model derived from all 23 stores. The predicted sales calculation in paragraph 3.60 differs slightly from the predicted sales calculation in exhibit 3-9 as a result of rounding.

Evaluating the Precision of the Regression Using R Squared, the t Statistic, and the Standard Error

3.62 The assessment of the precision of the regression is done by considering three statistical measures that are provided in the regression output.

3.63 In exhibit 3-9, R squared is excellent (at 97.5 percent), the standard error is reasonable ($97,961 is less than 5 percent of the average value of the dependent variable), and the t statistics are all greater than 2.0, except for Size, for which the t statistic is 1.198.

3.64 The standard error of $97,961 is substantially less than the planned materiality of $150,000, which provides further confidence in the use of the regression. In contrast, if the standard error is greater than roughly 75 percent of materiality, the auditor should consider limiting reliance on the regression.

3.65 Also the signs of the t statistics are in the expected direction. That is, each of the variables except variable 3 (a new store) is expected to have a positive relationship with the dependent variable: As the independent variable increases, the dependent variable is expected to increase. In contrast, for new stores, lower sales are expected, as indicated by the negative sign on variable 3. Thus, both the amount and direction of the t statistics are consistent with expectations. Overall, the precision of the regression is assessed to be quite good. The regression output contains additional information, but to obtain a concise and effective evaluation of the precision of the regression, the auditor can confine himself or herself at this point to a consideration of the three statistics noted previously.[1]

3.66 The auditor's overall evaluation then, is that the regression in exhibit 3-9 is useful, because the statistical measures are good. Also, because one of the variables, Size, has an insignificant t statistic, it could be removed from the regression to potentially improve the standard error and the t statistics of the remaining variables. This is done in exhibit 3-10. The standard error becomes slightly worse ($99,138 rather than $97,961), but the t statistics improve overall. Although judgment is involved, the auditor is likely to prefer the second regression in exhibit 3-10 because the relatively poor variable, Size, is removed, and the remaining t statistics are improved.

Identification, Investigation, and Evaluation (Phases II–IV)

3.67 To examine the stores for the completeness and existence of sales, the auditor first identifies stores with large prediction errors (labeled the *residuals* in the regression output), that is, the difference between the actual sales and predicted sales for each store. A common approach is to identify and focus on the largest few residuals. In particular, the auditor may choose all stores that have residuals greater than the standard error. The total number of stores to pick depends on the number of large residuals. The more stores with large residuals, the more stores should be selected to achieve the desired level of assurance.

3.68 Because the auditor in this case is looking for overstatements, the positive residuals are important; stores with positive residuals are those for which the regression predicts a lower level of sales than the actual number, a potential overstatement. Exhibit 3-10 shows that the largest positive residuals

[1] To further study the validity of the model, the regression can be run on a portion of the data and compared with the model for the entire data set. This was done using only the first 11 stores, and the results are comparable to that shown in exhibit 3-9. The statistical measures are similar to those in exhibit 3-9, except that across the board, all the measures are not as good (for example, the t statistics are 1.78, 2.32, -3.84, 4.30, and 2.09 for each of the independent variables respectively, in contrast to t statistics of 4.5, 5.98, -4.47, 8.49, and 1.198 in exhibit 3-9). The decline in the statistical measures is due largely to the relatively small number of data points. Generally, the larger the number of data points, the better the statistical measures will be.

are at store nos. 4, 8, and 18. The analysis points to beginning further investigation (if any) at stores 4, 8, and 18, because the regression shows them to be the most out of line with the other stores, based on the relationships in the data for these 4 independent variables.

3.69 Once the stores have been identified, the auditor begins a further analytical investigation. The goal of the additional analysis is to explain why these four stores are out of line in comparison with the others. The further analytics can be based on product line analysis or more detailed analysis of the predictor factors (that is, for new stores, how many months they were open). For example, On the Go Stores sales can be divided into the product lines: grocery and other merchandise, beer and wine, lottery, and gasoline. A more detailed analytical study can help explain why a store is out of line. For example, the analytics might show that store no. 8's sales are unusual because of an unusually large amount of sales of beer and wine. The explanations derived in this manner are then taken to management as a basis for inquiry, to corroborate the explanations found in the analytics or to discover new explanations. For example, management might respond that the unusual sales for store no. 8 are not likely due to beer and wine sales, but rather to a construction project near the store, which increased traffic at the store and increased sales significantly. Management's explanations should be corroborated by further analytics, inquiry, or testing.

Use of Regression in Review Engagements

3.70 Regression analysis can be used in the same manner for review engagements, to direct attention to accounts or to areas (that is, stores) where there is the greatest potential for misstatement.

Regression and Fraud Detection

3.71 Because of the potential for collusion in cases of fraud, the auditor cannot rely on regression to detect fraud. However, because of its precision, regression can sometimes be a useful resource for directing auditors' attention to potential fraud. To illustrate, assume there are no material errors at On the Go Stores, but there is a material fraud of $1,000,000 in which the management of On the Go has overstated net income by overstating sales by $1,000,000. The debit side of the misstatement is spread over selected balance sheet accounts. The credit side of the fraud is $250,000 spread over sales at each of the 4 stores: store nos. 4, 10, 12, and 22. On the Go's management chose these 4 stores because they have the lowest merchandise levels of the 23 stores, and their expectation was that the auditor was unlikely to select the stores with the smallest inventories for detail tests. The auditor has identified certain risk factors that indicate the potential for fraud and is planning to use regression as one part of the audit plan to satisfy the auditor's responsibility under AU-C section 240, *Consideration of Fraud in a Financial Statement Audit* (AICPA, *Professional Standards*), which is the primary source of authoritative guidance about an auditor's responsibilities concerning the consideration of fraud in a financial statement audit.

3.72 Paragraph .01 of AU section 316, *Consideration of Fraud in a Financial Statement Audit* (AICPA, *PCAOB Standards and Related Rules*, Interim Standards), states when performing an integrated audit of financial statements and internal control over financial reporting, refer to paragraphs 14–15 of PCAOB Auditing Standard No. 5, *An Audit of Internal Control Over Financial Reporting That Is Integrated with An Audit of Financial Statements*,

(AICPA, *PCAOB Standards and Related Rules*, Auditing Standards), regarding fraud considerations, in addition to the fraud considerations set forth in AU section 316.

3.73 The results of the regression (excluding the size variable), now including the fraud in the four stores, is shown in exhibit 3-11. Note that the R squared, standard error, and t statistics are still quite good, though the effect of the fraud is to reduce the overall precision of the regression slightly.[2] The analysis of the residuals shows the following. Suppose the auditor were to pick the 4 stores with the largest positive residuals to investigate for fraud. This strategy would pick store nos. 4, 8, 18, and 22. Two of the four (store nos. 4 and 22) have fraudulent sales, so the regression has correctly identified them as needing investigation. The regression also led to the choice of store nos. 8 and 18, for which there is no error or fraud. The unusually large residuals for store nos. 8 and 18 are likely due to factors not included in the regression—variables that would have caused these stores to have higher sales predictions if included—or other factors that are difficult to include in the regression such as turnover of management at the store or short-term personnel problems.[3]

3.74 The regression failed to identify store nos. 10 and 12 as needing investigation. Overall then, the score of the regression is two "hits," two "misses," and two "false alarms"—probably a good overall performance given that the fraud is spread over four stores. If the fraud is spread over more than four stores, the regression's model performance would be better. However, it is important to note that trend and ratio analysis or reasonableness testing are less precise and therefore less likely to reveal the fraud. For example, the next section examines how reasonableness testing would have performed in detecting this fraud.

---

[2] Although poor statistical measures are most likely due to modeling difficulties (missing independent variables, inaccurate data, and unstable data), it can also be due to fraud. The effect of the fraud is to reduce the explanatory power of the independent variables and therefore to make the statistical measures less favorable.

[3] There are two types of management fraud: (*a*) misstatement of the financial report (usually by top management), and (*b*) misappropriation of assets (theft, usually by lower level managers and employees). The application of regression illustrated here is the first type; the focus is on the discovery of overstatement. In contrast, if the objective is discovery of theft, the auditor would focus also on understatements and would therefore investigate those stores with large negative residuals. In exhibit 3-11, this would be store nos. 1, 3, 13, and 14.

Exhibit 3-11

Regression Results for the Fraud Data

SUMMARY OUTPUT

Regression Statistics	
Multiple R	0.966830033
R Squared	0.934760313
Adjusted R Squared	0.920262604
Standard Error	139385.2781
Observations	23

ANOVA

	df	*SS*	*MS*	*F*	*Significance F*
Regression	4	5.01066E+12	1.233E+12	64.476419	2.01524E-10
Residual	18	3.49709E+11	1.934E+09		
Total	22	5.36037E+12			

	Coefficients	*Standard Error*	*t Stat*	*P-Value*	*Lower 95%*	*Upper 95%*
Intercept	(652,163)	318,344	-2.049	0.055	(1,320,979)	16,653
Inventory	10.5906	5	2.207	0.041	1	21
FTE	123,287	24,252	5.084	0.000	72,336	174,238
New Store	(182,473)	88,169	-2.070	0.053	(367,709)	2,764
Sells Gas	893,157	89,108	10.023	0.000	705,949	1,080,365

RESIDUAL OUTPUT

Observation	*Predicted Sales*	*Residuals*
1	1,037,549	(255,756)
2	1,210,012	(63,574)
3	1,368,133	(173,129)
4	1,021,710	180,074
5	1,966,587	14,822
6	2,179,911	120,760
7	2,089,689	(133,208)
8	1,663,574	136,139
9	1,706,391	114,250
10	926,192	98,762
11	1,176,852	(17,848)
12	1,280,675	108,800
13	1,101,818	(153,296)
14	2,155,736	(170,959)
15	2,196,443	97,404
16	2,083,253	(98,531)
17	1,826,852	(28,516)
18	2,302,245	182,258
19	1,902,674	(65,274)

Observation	*Predicted Sales*	*Residuals*
20	1,604,104	5,281
21	1,934,403	(60,174)
22	818,117	130,216
23	1,166,729	31,500

Reasonableness Testing by Store

3.75 The reasonableness test based on square feet shown in exhibit 3-12 can be compared with the reasonableness test in exhibit 3-2. Store nos. 4, 10, and 22 may not be indicated for a fraud involving overstatement of revenues using this analysis because their sales-per-square-foot values ($300, $410, and $379, respectively) are below the national average of $490 per square foot in the first year of operation, which might be considered reasonable depending upon factors including the date operations began and market conditions in the area of the store.

Exhibit 3-12

Reasonableness Test Based on Sales per Square Foot With Fraud in Store Nos. 4, 10, 12, and 22

Store	*Square Foot*	*Sales*	*Sales/Square Foot*
13	4,000	948,522	237 New Store
4	4,000	1,201,784	300 New Store
1	2,500	781,793	313 New Store
22	2,500	948,333	379 New Store
20	4,000	1,609,385	402
10	2,500	1,024,954	410 New Store
14	4,000	1,609,385	402
17	4,000	1,798,336	450
8	4,000	1,799,713	450
9	4,000	1,820,641	455
2	2,500	1,146,438	459
19	4,000	1,837,400	459
11	2,500	1,159,004	464
21	4,000	1,874,229	469
3	2,500	1,195,004	478
23	2,500	1,198,229	479
7	4,000	1,956,481	489
5	4,000	1,981,409	495
16	4,000	1,984,722	496
14	4,000	1,984,777	496
12	2,500	1,389,475	556
15	4,000	2,293,847	573
6	4,000	2,300,671	575
18	4,000	2,484,503	621
Total	80,000	36,719,650	

3.76 Also, using this analysis in exhibit 3-2, store no. 12 has sales per square foot ($556) above the national average, but it is unlikely that it would be indicated for fraud using this approach because there are other stores that are further above the national average (store nos. 6, 15, and 18). Thus, it appears that the reasonableness testing approach based on individual stores, as illustrated in exhibit 3-12, probably would not be as effective as regression analysis at detecting the stores with fraud. This might be explained in part by the lack of significance of the size (square feet) variable in exhibit 3-9. Because size did not appear as a significant variable in the regression, square footage may not be a reliable basis for forming an expectation about store sales in this case.

Appendix A

Measures of Precision for a Regression Analysis

A.01 Unlike trend and ratio analysis or reasonableness testing, which provide no direct measures of the precision of their expectations, regression analysis provides direct, quantitative measures of the precision of its expectation. Many computer-based statistical software systems, such as Excel (used in this example), provide these measures as part of the regression results. There are three key measures of precision provided in the regression:

a. R squared

b. The t statistic

c. The standard error of the estimate

A.02 R squared is a number between 0 and 1 and measures the degree to which changes in the dependent variable can be estimated by changes in the independent variable(s). A more precise regression is one that has a relatively high R squared (close to 1). When viewed graphically, models with high R squared show the data points lying near to the regression line, whereas in low R squared models, the data points are somewhat dispersed, as demonstrated in exhibit A-1 and exhibit A-2. Determining an acceptable R squared is a matter of judgment; most regression analyses involving financial data have R squared values above .5, and many have values in the .8 to .9 range.

Exhibit A-1

Regression With High R Squared

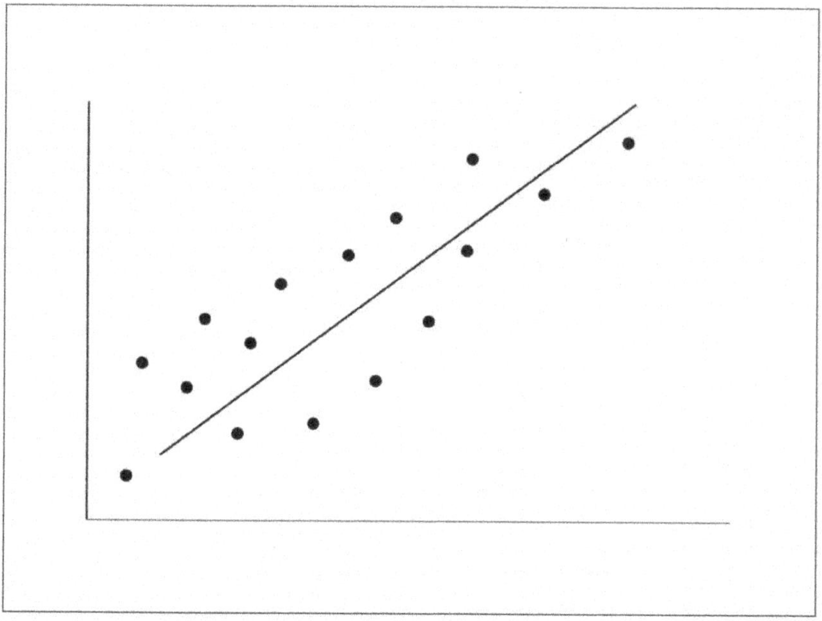

Exhibit A-2

Regression With Low R Squared

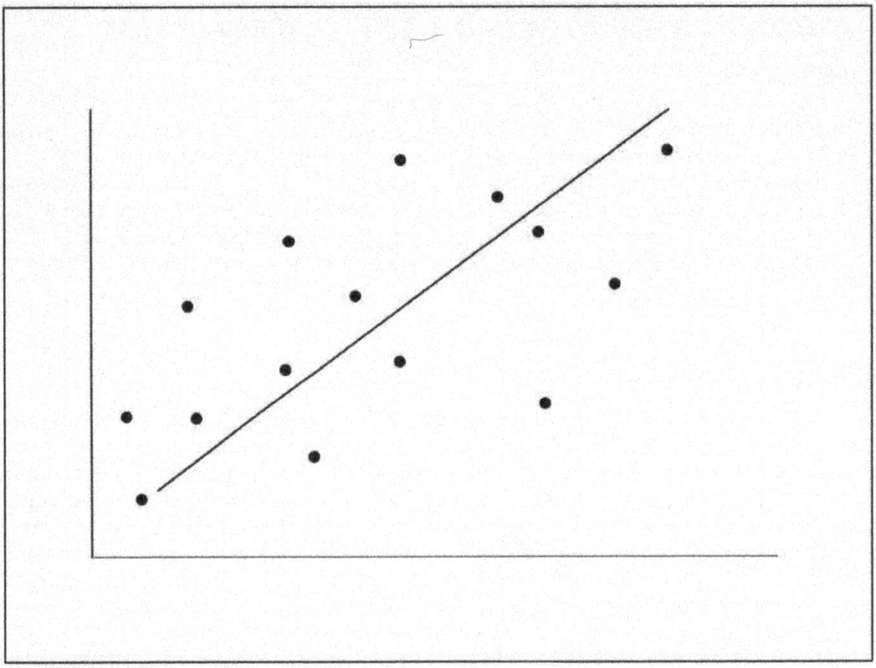

A.03 The t statistic is interpreted very much like R squared. It is a measure of the degree to which each independent variable has a valid relationship with the dependent variable. A relatively small t statistic (although it is a matter of judgment, many auditors look for the t statistic to be greater than 1.3, which translates to an approximately 80 percent confidence level) is an indication of little or no relationship between the independent and dependent variable. When the t statistic is relatively low, the auditor might consider removing that variable from the regression.

A.04 Also, the presence of a low t statistic on one or more of the independent variables is a common signal of what is called multicollinearity, which is present when two or more independent variables are highly correlated with each other. Correlation among variables, like R squared, means that a given variable tends to change predictably in the same (or opposite) direction for a given change in the other variable. Because there tend to be trends affecting many types of financial time-series data, it is common for accounting and operating data to be highly correlated. The effect of this condition is that the predictions of the regression might be less accurate. In particular, multicollinearity tends to cause understatement of the t statistics relating to the correlated independent variables. Thus, when the auditor has reason to believe that two or more of the independent variables are correlated, and the auditor observes relatively low t statistics, then the auditor might consider removing one or more of the correlated variables. One common approach in this situation is to perform a number of regression analyses with alternative combinations of the independent variables, and examine the different effects on R squared and the t statistics. To facilitate this, many software programs, such as Excel, can report the "correlation matrix," which shows directly the degree of correlation between each pair of independent variables.

A.05 The standard error (SE) of the estimate is a measure of the accuracy of the regression's estimates. It is a measure of the range around the regression line in which auditors can be reasonably sure that the unknown actual value will fall. For example, if the auditor predicts that an amount will be $4,500 for a regression having an SE of $500, then the auditor can estimate with reasonable confidence that the unknown actual value lies somewhere in the range $4,500 +/– (1.3 x $500), or $3,850 to $5,150.[1] Good and poor values for the standard error are illustrated in exhibits A-3 and A-4.

Exhibit A-3

Regression With Narrow (Good) Standard Error

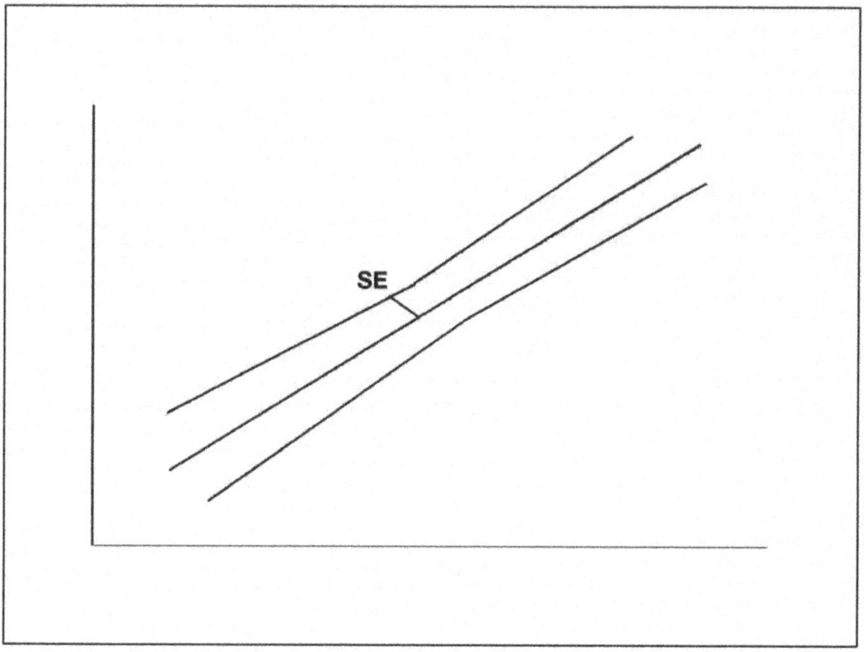

---

[1] Multiplying the standard error by 1.3 in this calculation yields approximately an 80 percent confidence interval. If the auditor desires a different confidence level, a different multiplier is simply substituted in the calculation of the confidence interval. For example, a multiplier of 1.0 yields approximately a 67 percent confidence interval. For a 95 percent confidence level, the auditor would substitute a multiplier of 2.0 in the calculation.

Exhibit A-4

Regression With Wide (Poor) Standard Error

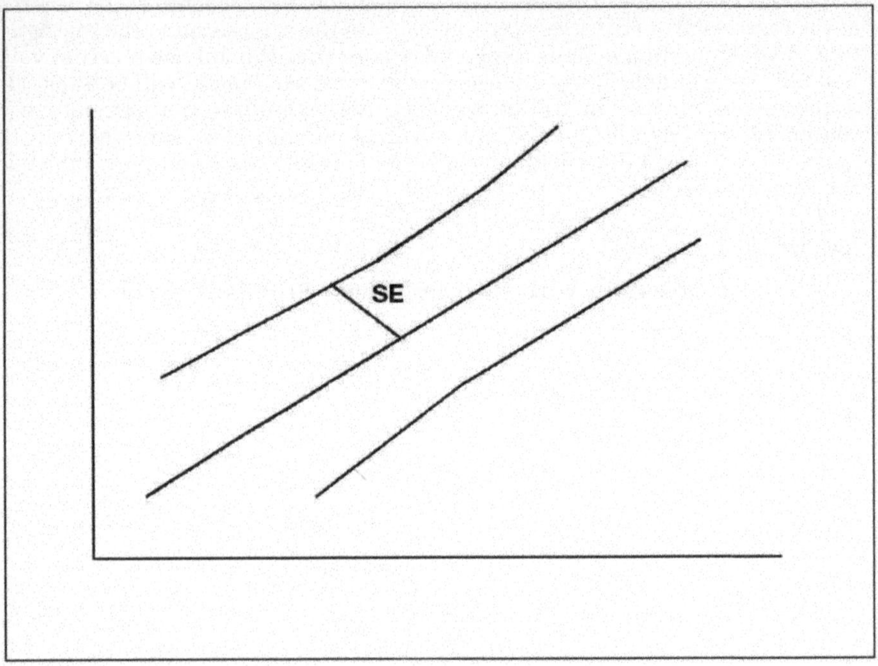

A.06 Because it is used to measure a range, the SE is interpreted in terms of its relationship to the average amount of the dependent variable. If the SE is small relative to the dependent variable, the precision of the model can be assessed as relatively good. How small the SE value has to be relative to the mean of the dependent variable for a favorable precision evaluation is a matter of judgement, but often the threshold of 10 percent is suggested.

Appendix B

Financial Ratios

In the following table are several financial ratios that may be helpful while performing some of the analytical procedures contained in this guide. These financial ratios include liquidity, activity, and efficiency ratios.

Financial Ratios	*Formula*	*Explanation*
Current Ratio	$\frac{\text{Current Assets}}{\text{Current Liabilities}}$	Measures ability to meet short term obligations
Quick Ratio (or Acid Test Ratio)	$\frac{\text{Current Assets—Inventory}}{\text{Current Liabilities}}$	A more conservative measure of an entity's ability to meet short term obligations
Operating Cash Flows to Current Liabilities	$\frac{\text{Cash Provided by Operations}}{\text{Average Current Liabilities}}$	Liquidity calculation
Days Sales in Accounts Receivable	$\frac{\text{Net Accounts Receivable}}{\text{Net Sales/360}}$	Measures length of time average sales is a receivable
Allowance for Bad Credit as a % of Accounts Receivable	$\frac{\text{Allowance for Bad Debt}}{\text{Accounts Receivable}}$	Calculation is compared to prior periods and other comparable entities
Bad Debt Expense as a % of Net Sales	$\frac{\text{Bad Debt Expense}}{\text{Net Sales}}$	Calculation is compared to prior periods and other comparable entities
Inventory Turnover	$\frac{\text{Cost of Sales}}{\text{Inventory}}$	Activity ratio—indication of efficiency of operation
Fixed Asset Turnover	$\frac{\text{Net sales}}{\text{Average Fixed Assets}}$	Activity ratio
Receivable Turnover	$\frac{\text{Net Credit Sales}}{\text{Average Receivables}}$	Activity ratio
Net Sales to Inventory	$\frac{\text{Net sales}}{\text{Inventory}}$	Activity ratio

(continued)

Financial Ratios	*Formula*	*Explanation*
Days in Inventory	$\frac{\text{Inventory X (Days in a Cycle)}}{\text{Cost of Sales}}$	Identifies how many days of inventory is available
Accounts Payable to Net Sales	$\frac{\text{Accounts Payable X (Days in a cycle)}}{\text{Net Sales X (Days in a year)}}$	Compares A/P balance to net sales
Return on Total Assets	$\frac{\text{Earnings Before Income Tax (EBIT)}}{\text{Total Net Assets}}$	Identifies effective use of assets to generate earnings
Return on Net Worth	$\frac{\text{Net Income X (Days in a year)}}{\text{Net Worth X (Days in a cycle)}}$	Profitability measure
Return on Net Sales	$\frac{\text{Net Income}}{\text{Net Sales}}$	Profit margin
Net Sales to Accounts Receivable	$\frac{\text{Net Sales X (Days in a year)}}{\text{Net Accounts Receivable X (Days in a cycle)}}$	Identifies how many times Accounts Receivable will turn over per year of the operating cycle
Net Sales to Net Fixed Assets	$\frac{\text{Net Sales X (Days in a year)}}{\text{Fixed Assets X (Days in a cycle)}}$	Identifies efficiency of capital investment
Income Before Tax to Net Worth	$\frac{\text{Earnings Before Income Tax (EBIT) X (Days in a year)}}{\text{Net Worth X (Days in a cycle)}}$	Ratio of earnings to net worth per year
Gross Profit Percentage	$\frac{\text{Net Sales} - \text{Cost of Sales}}{\text{Net Sales}}$	Profitability calculation
Operating Expenses as a % of Net Sales	$\frac{\text{Operating Expenses}}{\text{Net Sales}}$	Efficiency calculation

Appendix C

Mapping and Summarization of Changes—Clarified Auditing Standards

This appendix maps the extant[1] AU sections to the clarified AU-C sections. As a result of the Auditing Standards Board's (ASB's) Clarity Project, all extant AU sections have been modified. In some cases, individual AU sections have been revised into individual clarified standards. In other cases, some AU sections have been grouped together and revised as one or more clarified standards. In addition, the ASB revised the AU section number order established by Statement on Auditing Standards No. 1, *Responsibilities and Functions of the Independent Auditor* (AICPA, *Professional Standards*, AU sec. 110), to follow the same number order used in International Standards on Auditing (ISAs) for all clarified AU sections for which there are comparable ISAs. The clarified standards are effective for periods ending on or after December 15, 2012. Early adoption is not permitted.

Although the Clarity Project was not intended to create additional requirements, some revisions have resulted in changes that may require auditors to make adjustments in their practices. To assist auditors in the transition process, these changes have been organized into the following four types:

- Substantive changes
- Primarily clarifying changes
- Primarily formatting changes
- Standards not yet issued in the Clarity Project

This appendix identifies those AU-C sections associated with these four types of changes.

Substantive Changes

Substantive changes are considered likely to affect the firms' audit methodology and engagements because they contain *substantive* or *other changes*, defined as having one or both of the following characteristics:

- A change or changes to an audit methodology that may require effort to implement
- A number of small changes that, although not individually significant, may affect audit engagements

Primarily Clarifying Changes

Primarily clarifying changes are intended to explicitly state what may have been implicit in the extant standards, which, over time, resulted in diversity in practice.

---

[1] The term *extant* is used throughout this appendix in reference to the standards that are superseded by the clarified standards.

Primarily Formatting Changes

Primarily formatting changes from the extant standards do not contain changes that expand the extant sections in any significant way and may not require adjustments to current practice.

Standards Not Yet Issued in the Clarity Project

Standards not yet issued in the Clarity Project contain the remaining sections that are in exposure or have not yet been reworked.

The preface of this guide and the Financial Reporting Center at www.aicpa.org/InterestAreas/FRC/Pages/FRC.aspx provide more information about the Clarity Project. You can also visit www.aicpa.org/InterestAreas/FRC/AuditAttest/Pages/ImprovingClarityASBStandards.aspx.

Extant AU Sections Mapped to the Clarified AU-C Sections

Extant AU Section		AU Section Superseded	New AU-C Section		Type of Change
110	Responsibilities and Functions of the Independent Auditor	All	200	Overall Objectives of the Independent Auditor and the Conduct of an Audit in Accordance With Generally Accepted Auditing Standards [1]	Primarily formatting changes
120	Defining Professional Requirements in Statements on Auditing Standards	All			
150	Generally Accepted Auditing Standards	All			
161	The Relationship of Generally Accepted Auditing Standards to Quality Control Standards	All	220	Quality Control for an Engagement Conducted in Accordance With Generally Accepted Auditing Standards	Primarily clarifying changes
201	Nature of the General Standards	All	200	Overall Objectives of the Independent Auditor and the Conduct of an Audit in Accordance With Generally Accepted Auditing Standards [1]	Primarily formatting changes
210	Training and Proficiency of the Independent Auditor	All			
220	Independence	All			
230	Due Professional Care in the Performance of Work	All			
311	Planning and Supervision	All except paragraphs .08–.10	300	Planning an Audit	Primarily formatting changes
		Paragraphs .08–.10	210	Terms of Engagement	Primarily clarifying changes
312	Audit Risk and Materiality in Conducting an Audit	All	320	Materiality in Planning and Performing an Audit	Primarily formatting changes
			450	Evaluation of Misstatements Identified During the Audit	Primarily formatting changes

(continued)

Extant AU Section		AU Section Superseded	New AU-C Section		Type of Change
314	Understanding the Entity and Its Environment and Assessing the Risks of Material Misstatement	All	315	Understanding the Entity and Its Environment and Assessing the Risks of Material Misstatement	Primarily formatting changes
315	Communications Between Predecessor and Successor Auditors	All except paragraphs .03–.10 and .14	510	Opening Balances—Initial Audit Engagements, Including Reaudit Engagements	Primarily clarifying changes
		Paragraphs .03–.10 and .14	210	Terms of Engagement	Primarily clarifying changes
316	Consideration of Fraud in a Financial Statement Audit	All	240	Consideration of Fraud in a Financial Statement Audit	Primarily formatting changes
317	Illegal Acts by Clients	All	250	Consideration of Laws and Regulations in an Audit of Financial Statements	Substantive changes
318	Performing Audit Procedures in Response to Assessed Risks and Evaluating the Audit Evidence Obtained	All	330	Performing Audit Procedures in Response to Assessed Risks and Evaluating the Audit Evidence Obtained	Primarily formatting changes
322	The Auditor's Consideration of the Internal Audit Function in an Audit of Financial Statements	All	Planned to be issued as AU-C section 610	The Auditor's Consideration of the Internal Audit Function in an Audit of Financial Statements	Standards not yet issued in the Clarity Project
324	Service Organizations	All	402	Audit Considerations Relating to an Entity Using a Service Organization	Primarily clarifying changes
325	Communicating Internal Control Related Matters Identified in an Audit	All	265	Communicating Internal Control Related Matters Identified in an Audit	Substantive changes

Extant AU Section		AU Section Superseded	New AU-C Section		Type of Change
326	Audit Evidence	All	500	Audit Evidence	Primarily formatting changes
328	Auditing Fair Value Measurements and Disclosures	All	540	Auditing Accounting Estimates, Including Fair Value Accounting Estimates, and Related Disclosures [2]	Primarily formatting changes
329	Analytical Procedures	All	520	Analytical Procedures	Primarily formatting changes
330	The Confirmation Process	All	505	External Confirmations	Primarily clarifying changes
331	Inventories	All	501	Audit Evidence—Specific Considerations for Selected Items [3]	Primarily clarifying changes
332	Auditing Derivative Instruments, Hedging Activities, and Investments in Securities	All	501	Audit Evidence—Specific Considerations for Selected Items [3]	Primarily clarifying changes
333	Management Representations	All	580	Written Representations	Primarily formatting changes
334	Related Parties	All	550	Related Parties	Substantive changes
336	Using the Work of a Specialist	All	620	Using the Work of an Auditor's Specialist	Primarily Clarifying Changes
337	Inquiry of a Client's Lawyer Concerning Litigation, Claims, and Assessments	All	501	Audit Evidence—Specific Considerations for Selected Items [3]	Primarily clarifying changes
339	Audit Documentation	All	230	Audit Documentation	Primarily formatting changes

(continued)

Extant AU Section		AU Section Superseded	New AU-C Section		Type of Change
341	The Auditor's Consideration of an Entity's Ability to Continue as a Going Concern	All	Planned to be issued as AU-C section 570	Going Concern (in exposure)	Standards not yet issued in the Clarity Project
342	Auditing Accounting Estimates	All	540	Auditing Accounting Estimates, Including Fair Value Accounting Estimates, and Related Disclosures [2]	Primarily formatting changes
350	Audit Sampling	All	530	Audit Sampling	Primarily formatting changes
380	The Auditor's Communication With Those Charged With Governance	All	260	The Auditor's Communication With Those Charged With Governance	Primarily formatting changes
390	Consideration of Omitted Procedures After the Report Date	All	585	Consideration of Omitted Procedures After the Report Release Date	Primarily formatting changes
410	Adherence to Generally Accepted Accounting Principles	All	700	Forming an Opinion and Reporting on Financial Statements [4]	Substantive changes
420	Consistency of Application of Generally Accepted Accounting Principles	All	708	Consistency of Financial Statements	Primarily clarifying changes
431	Adequacy of Disclosure in Financial Statements	All	705	Modifications to the Opinion in the Independent Auditor's Report [5]	Primarily formatting changes
504	Association With Financial Statements	All	N/A	Withdrawn	

Extant AU Section		AU Section Superseded	New AU-C Section		Type of Change
508	Reports on Audited Financial Statements	Paragraphs .01–.11, .14–.15, .19–.32, .35–.52, .58–.70, and .74–.76	700	Forming an Opinion and Reporting on Financial Statements [4]	Substantive changes
			705	Modifications to the Opinion in the Independent Auditor's Report [5]	Primarily formatting changes
			706	Emphasis-of-Matter Paragraphs and Other-Matter Paragraphs in the Independent Auditor's Report [6]	Substantive changes
		Paragraphs .12–.13	600	Special Considerations—Audits of Group Financial Statements (Including the Work of Component Auditors)	Substantive changes
		Paragraphs .16–.18 and .53–.57	708	Consistency of Financial Statements	Primarily clarifying changes
		Paragraphs .33–.34	805	Special Considerations—Audits of Single Financial Statements and Specific Elements, Accounts, or Items of a Financial Statement	Primarily clarifying changes
		Paragraphs .71–.73	560	Subsequent Events and Subsequently Discovered Facts [7]	Primarily formatting changes

(continued)

Extant AU Section		AU Section Superseded	New AU-C Section		Type of Change
530	Dating of the Independent Auditor's Report	Paragraphs .01–.02	700	Forming an Opinion and Reporting on Financial Statements [4]	Substantive changes
		Paragraphs .03–.08	560	Subsequent Events and Subsequently Discovered Facts [7]	Primarily formatting changes
532	Restricting the Use of an Auditor's Report	All	905	Alert That Restricts the Use of the Auditor's Written Communication	Primarily clarifying changes
534	Reporting on Financial Statements Prepared for Use in Other Countries	All	910	Financial Statements Prepared in Accordance With a Financial Reporting Framework Generally Accepted in Another Country	Primarily clarifying changes
543	Part of Audit Performed by Other Independent Auditors	All	600	Special Considerations—Audits of Group Financial Statements (Including the Work of Component Auditors)	Substantive changes
544	Lack of Conformity With Generally Accepted Accounting Principles	All	800	Special Considerations—Audits of Financial Statements Prepared in Accordance With Special Purpose Frameworks [8]	Primarily clarifying changes
550	Other Information in Documents Containing Audited Financial Statements	All	720	Other Information in Documents Containing Audited Financial Statements	Primarily formatting changes

Extant AU Section		AU Section Superseded	New AU-C Section		Type of Change
551	Supplementary Information in Relation to the Financial Statements as a Whole	All	725	Supplementary Information in Relation to the Financial Statements as a Whole	Primarily formatting changes
552	Reporting on Condensed Financial Statements and Selected Financial Data	All	810	Engagements to Report on Summary Financial Statements	Primarily clarifying changes
558	Required Supplementary Information	All	730	Required Supplementary Information	Primarily formatting changes
560	Subsequent Events	All	560	Subsequent Events and Subsequently Discovered Facts [7]	Primarily formatting changes
561	Subsequent Discovery of Facts Existing at the Date of the Auditor's Report	All			
623	Special Reports	Paragraphs .19–.21	806	Reporting on Compliance With Aspects of Contractual Agreements or Regulatory Requirements in Connection With Audited Financial Statements	Primarily formatting changes
		Paragraphs .01–.10 and .22–.34	800	Special Considerations—Audits of Financial Statements Prepared in Accordance With Special Purpose Frameworks [8]	Primarily clarifying changes
		Paragraphs .11–.18	805	Special Considerations—Audits of Single Financial Statements and Specific Elements, Accounts, or Items of a Financial Statement	Primarily clarifying changes

(continued)

Extant AU Section		AU Section Superseded	New AU-C Section		Type of Change
625	Reports on the Application of Accounting Principles	All	915	Reports on Application of Requirements of an Applicable Financial Reporting Framework	Primarily formatting changes
634	Letters for Underwriters and Certain Other Requesting Parties	All	920	Letters for Underwriters and Certain Other Requesting Parties	Primarily formatting changes
711	Filings Under Federal Securities Statutes	All	925	Filings With the U.S. Securities and Exchange Commission Under the Securities Act of 1933	Primarily formatting changes
722	Interim Financial Information	All	930	Interim Financial Information	Primarily formatting changes
801	Compliance Audits	All	935	Compliance Audits	Primarily formatting changes
901	Public Warehouses—Controls and Auditing Procedures for Goods Held	All	501	Audit Evidence—Specific Considerations for Selected Items [3]	Primarily clarifying changes

Legend:

[n] Bracketed number indicates a clarity standard that supersedes more than one extant AU section.

The AICPA has developed an Audit Risk Alert to assist auditors and members in practice prepare for the transition to the clarified standards. It has been organized to give you the background information on the development of the clarified standards and to identify the new requirements and changes from the extant standards. Check out the Audit Risk Alert *Understanding the Clarified Auditing Standards* (product no. ARACLA12P), which is available in the AICPA store on www.cpa2biz.com.

Appendix D

Schedule of Changes Made to the Text From the Previous Edition

As of March 1, 2012

This schedule of changes identifies areas in the text and footnotes of this guide that have that have changed since the previous edition. Entries in the table of this appendix reflect current numbering, lettering (including that in appendix names), and character designations that resulted from the renumbering or reordering that occurred in the updating of this guide.

Reference	*Change*
General	Guidance related to the clarified auditing standards (Statement on Auditing Standards Nos. 122–125) has been incorporated throughout this guide. See the preface to this guide and appendix C, "Mapping and Summarization of Changes—Clarified Auditing Standards," for information on the clarifying changes to the extant standards resulting from the Clarity Project.
General	The use of footnotes denoted with a symbol instead of a number (referred to as "temporary" footnotes) has been discontinued. All content in such footnotes has been added to chapter text, converted to a numbered footnote, or deleted.
Preface	Updated.
Appendix C	Added.
Former appendixes C and D	Deleted for passage of time.